めぐる、めくる、めくるめく

石川県立図書館の新世界

仙田 満 +
環境デザイン研究所編

Mitsuru Senda +
Environment Design Institute

Explore, Encounter, Experience
Discovering the World of Ishikawa Prefectural Library

図書館南西角側の外観。外壁のコンクリートパネルが二次曲面となっており、本をめくるイメージを表現している。

文化交流エリアより閲覧エリア、グレートホールへ。
この空間に入ると多くの人が天井を見上げる。

S
南 SOUTH
E
東 EAST
BEING CURIOUS
【好奇心を抱く】 BEING CURIOUS
LA CURIOSITÉ

【好奇心を抱く】BEING CURIOUS

7万冊が一望できるグレートホール。面陳された本の合間に12の
サインが浮かび上がる。段状のラウンジは1〜3階のスロープに
連結しており、新たな本との出会いに誘う。

グレートホールの天井。単層ラメラドームの構造を見る。

目次 Contents

ワンダリングと集中
Wandering and Concentration

歩き回ることは脳を活性化させる。そして興味のあることに集中する。
来訪者にとって歩き回りやすい空間、集中しやすい場の両方が必要だ。
それが石川県立図書館の中心的なテーマである。

好奇心の海を泳ぐ
Swimming in a Sea of Curiosity

本館の利用者による新聞寄稿に
「本を探すというより、好奇心の海を泳ぐように歩き回った」と記されていた。
「遊環構造」の図書空間のあり方が的確に表現されていることに感動した。

グレートホール
Great Hall

多くの利用者にとって、ここに居て、本を読み、
学ぶことの一体感と共感を得られる空間をグレートホールと呼ぶ。
「遊環構造」における中心的で
感動的な「めまいの空間」である。

工芸建築
Kogei Architecture

工芸県・石川の建築として、美術工芸的な技を
表現するエレベーションを模索した。
結果的に外壁の乾式タイルに色、彫、影を施し、
深みのある建築が完成した。

知の庭園／知の広場／知の殿堂／知のアリーナ
Garden of Knowledge / Plaza of Knowledge / Hall of Knowledge / Arena of Knowledge

図書館を「知の庭園」と呼んだのは文学者の松浦寿輝。
イタリアの図書館学者アンニョリはイタリアの目指すべき図書館を「知の広場」と名づけた。
石川県立図書館は基本構想段階から「知の殿堂」を目指してきた。
私はグレートホールを知と出会い、知と闘う「知のアリーナ」と呼んでいる。

めぐる、めくる、めくるめく
Explore, Encounter, Experience

歩き回ることによって、
本をめくるように新しい世界に没入し、深い感情を呼び覚ます。
そのような石川県立図書館の空間的な展開を、
三つの台詞による言葉遊びで表現した。

目次空間
Space with a Table of Contents

図書館にも本の目次やグラビアのように"目次空間"が必要だ。
それが利用者にとって、本館をわかりやすく、楽しくしてくれている。

遊環構造
Circular Play System

意欲を喚起する空間の構造として1984年に発表した「遊環構造」のモデル図は、
国際教養大学図書館や広島市民球場において「めまい空間」が中心となった（右図）。
フランスの社会学者ロジェ・カイヨワの「めまい」の定義を、
多くの人々が一体感を持つ「まつり」の高揚感のような感情にまで拡大した。
「めまい空間」を中心に回遊と多様な体験空間が取りついている石川県立図書館は、
その新たな遊環構造モデルの最新作品である。

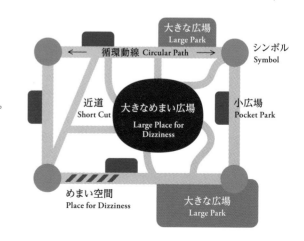

を楽しむキーワード

尚

Help You Enjoy Ishikawa Prefectural Library

ダブルD字体
Double D Structure

文化交流エリアと閲覧エリアを合体させるため、
国際教養大学図書館で実現した平面的D字体を
二つ重ね合わせたものが石川県立図書館のグレートホールである。
円形ではなく、ダブルD字体により構成される長円形だ。

公園のような図書館
A Library like a Park

プロポーザル時に「悲しい時も、うれしい時も、困難な時も、
毎日のように公園を散歩し、心を癒し、元気を取り戻している」という、
妻と息子を亡くした友人の記事を読んだ。
そんな、公園のような図書館をつくりたいと考えた。

ユニバーサルデザイン／インクルーシブデザイン建築
Architecture with Universal / Inclusive Design

1階から3階までスロープで繋ぐユニバーサルデザインの徹底がテーマであった。
障がい者施設での実験、原寸モックアップモデルの確認、
現地地下での最終検査、車椅子利用者の方々の参加、確認を経て、
スロープの幅、勾配、手すり等の寸法、ディテールを決定した。

気がついたら8時間
Not Noticing Eight Hours Passing

取材してくれた読売新聞の記者が
「気がついたら8時間も図書館にいた」と書いてくれた。
この図書館が、多様な場所で多様な本に出会い、
人々が居続けられる場となっているということなのだろう。

グッド・サーキュラー・プレイス
Good Circular Place

「遊環構造」は単なる回遊性でなく、
歩き回っていくことによって高位の段階に上昇し、循環性を得る。
本を何度も読むことによって、より深い真理を見出すことができるように、
来訪者にとって、そのような好循環の場として
石川県立図書館が存在することを期待したい。

隙間の居場所
Interspace Where One Can Fit In

タイルパネルが貼られた外壁は2、3階を覆っており、
その隙間の内側には小さな半個室的な空間が形成されている。
グレートホールに向かう中心的な空間ではなく、外の緑の環境に向かう窓を有している。

入れ子構造
Nested Structure

敷地の中央部に建物は位置し、その周辺を駐車場、緑地が取り巻く。
四角い平面の外形に対して、
内部の中央には長円形のグレートホールが置かれ、
同心円状の回遊路に多様な機能空間が接続し、
内外を人々が行き来する入れ子の構造となっている。

面陳の力
Power of Face-Out Display

石川県立図書館では書棚で本の表紙を見せる
「面陳」という展示手法がとられている。
これがグレートホールの長円形の段状空間を歩き回る
機動力になっているに違いない。

ラメラドーム
Lamella Dome

グレートホールの天井はトップサイドライトにより、外光をやさしく招き入れる。
この前田家の成巽閣を引用した群青色の空間は50mのスパンを持つ、
大きなラメラドームにより支持されている。
この図書館に入る多くの人が必ずこのラメラドームを見上げ、
スマホのシャッターを押す。

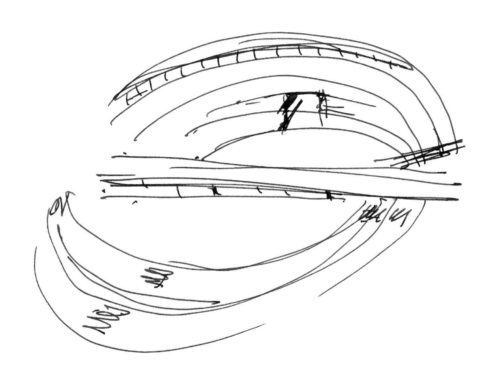

めぐる　　公園のように本の奇心のままに環る.
めくる.　　本をめくる.壁をめくる.新しい知の出会いに期待する.
めくるめく.　楽しく感動する.内内と空間を共有し共感する.

仙田　満

I

Book Arena

グレートホールを備え、来館者を圧倒する図書館とは？

What is a library that overwhelms visitors with its Great Hall?

亀井 優
Yu KAMEI

清水建設 北陸支店建築部
工事長

金箱温春
Yoshiharu KANEBAKO

金箱構造設計事務所
代表取締役

仙田 満
Mitsuru SENDA

環境デザイン研究所会長

来館者が一目で驚かされるのが、本をめくる形状を表した巨大な外壁パネルと、
閲覧エリアを包み込む大空間「グレートホール」の存在だ。
超高難度の技術を駆使した（清水建設・亀井氏）という石川県立図書館の主要部分の
構造設計と施工について、その工程を振り返ってもらった。

The visitors to this library are instantly blown away at the sight of the huge outer wall panels that capture pages of a book
being flipped, and the "Great Hall," an enormous space encapsulating the reading area.
We asked the people behind the structural design and construction of the main part of Ishikawa Prefectural Library
about the process of these "most advanced technological challenges" (as Mr. Kamei from Shimizu Corporation describes).

軽やかな「ラメラドーム」が実現するまで

How We Realized the Delicate "Lamella Dome"

仙田　15年ほど前、私は半円形の平面の図書館をつくりました。それは国際教養大学で初めて試みたもので"ブックコロシアム"と名づけました。半円にすることによって視線がクローズしないで繋がるのですが、今回もプロポーザルの時にそういう意識がありました。いわゆる市民広場的なものと図書館的な空間という二つの核を考えていたのですが、それを基本設計の際に重ね合わせたわけです。半円というものにこだわりながら、それを二つ合わせて、全体としては1核にしようと試みました。

これが自分自身でもうまくいったなと思うのは、屋内広場から図書スペースのアプローチに入っていくと、段裏の空間が段々低くなっていって、真ん中でドンと広がるような感覚をもたらすような空間演出が実現できたことです。この建物を訪れた人は皆、図書館の領域に入った瞬間に上を向くんですね。小さな空間から急に大きな空間に入っていって、天井を見ると「ドン！」という新鮮な驚きを与えることができているんですね。

いわゆる構造的には、金箱さんに手がけていただいた「ラメラドーム」と呼ばれるもので、直径が40～50mという大きな空間です。それが"軽やか"にでき上がっていることを皆、不思議がるんですよね。

金箱　おっしゃるように、最初二つだった閲覧室が一体になりました。当初は半円の組み合わせということで、ブリッジを使って屋根を支えるという発想で検討を進めていたのですが、どうしても空間の中に下から支えにいくものが出てくるとすっきりしないので、ブリッジとは切り離して考えようということになりました。

見上げるとドーム状の空間なのですが、屋根はフラットです。そこで最初はドームではなくて、張弦梁のような構造を考えていたんです。なぜかというと建物の壁が立ち上がっていて、その上に屋根を乗せた時に、張弦梁であればスラストは生じませんが、ドームではしっかりした下部構造により、スラストを抑えないといけないからです。また、平面的には正円でなく楕円形なので、純粋なドームにはなれないわけです。そうすると下部構造に負担をかけないようにするためには、トラス的なものや張弦梁のようなものを使う方がよいということで途中まで進めていたのですが、仙田先生がどうしてもドーム状の空間にしたいということで(笑)、ある時点からドーム状の構造を目指し、「ラメラドーム」に行きつきました。

ラメラというのはひし形のことです。普通ドームには水平のリング状部材があって、それが桶のタガを留めるみたいな効果をもたらしています。つまり三角形のグリッドですが、水平材をやめると非常に面白いかたちができる。アーチが放射状に並んで、それが少し変形しているという架構なんですね。

それから、スラストをどうやって留めるかということになるのですが、柱が壁の少し内側にあって、アーチ材が柱に繋がり、反対側に伸びて

Senda: About 15 years ago, I first experimented with my semicircular plan for a library at Akita International University, which I later named "Book Colosseum." A semicircular design connects sight lines rather than closing them, and that was what I was thinking when I made the proposal for this new library as well. At first, I was thinking of designing two cores, one acting as a public square and another as a library area, which I combined into one at the schematic design phase. Here, I attempted to stick to the semicircular formula, while using two of them to make a single-core space as a whole.

I am particularly happy with how the space dramatically shows up, when you enter the library from the Indoor Square, through the approach under the steps lowering in height, and once you reach the center, the whole space opens up. When you first visit the building, and enter the library area, everyone looks up. You go through small spaces into suddenly a large one, and if you look up, "boom!" it gives you this surprise.

Mr. Kanebako designed the structure of the space, called the "lamella dome," with a huge diameter of 40 to 50 meters. Everyone wonders how we managed to make it so "delicate."

Kanebako: Yes, there were two reading rooms in the initial design, which later became one space. Our first thought was to use the Bridge to support the roof that was a combination of semicircles, but having supports from below inside the space wasn't elegant, so we decided to separate the Bridge from the roof structure.

The shape of the space is a dome if you look from inside, but in fact the roof is flat. So we started from a beam string structure, not a dome because when you place a roof on top of the building's walls, a beam string structure does not generate thrust, but a dome requires a rigid lower structure to suppress the thrust.

Moreover, the plan was not a regular circle but an ellipse, which meant the roof could not be a simple dome. That was why until some point we proceeded with trusses or beam string structures to avoid stress on the lower structure, but since Mr. Senda insisted on a dome shape (laughs), we shifted our focus on the dome structure and came up with the lamella dome.

A lamella structure means it has diamond patterns. An ordinary dome has horizontal rings that tighten the structure like hoops of a bucket, resulting in triangular grids. But if you remove these horizontal elements, an interesting pattern appears. Our structure has arches arrayed radially, and slightly transformed.

Then we had to somehow resist the thrust. We placed posts a bit inward from the walls, and connected them to the arches, which then reached towards the other ends, where they formed a ring at the lower part of the roof to retain the dome in a unique composition. This structure bears the load axially, which contributes to the delicate impression.

The elliptic shape also adds to the interest. A regular circle would have a

いって、最終的には低い部分の屋根でリングが形成されて、それでドームが成り立っているという特殊な構成なんです。軸力で力が伝達する構造なので、それで"軽やかさ"が出たのではないかと思います。あとは楕円であるということの面白さですね。正円の場合はグリッドの形状が繰り返されるのですが、楕円なので、見るところによって少しずつ形も大きさも違うので、それが視覚的な魅力に繋がっているのではないかと。ともかく軽やかにできているのは、やはりドームの形を活かそうということと、ドームだけどタイプループというか、桶のタガのような水平材を使わなかったという、その二つが大きかったのかなと思いますね。

仙田　ここを「グレートホール」と呼んでいるのですが、7万冊が一度に見える空間で、屋根を非常にうまくつくることができたわけです。軽やかな空間の構造と、色彩的にも成巽閣という前田家の書院造の建物から引用して、ブルーに塗らせてもらった効果が非常に大きいですね。

金箱　ドームの色と、上部の青色の対比が効いていますよね。
先ほどの話の補足ですが、この軽やかな構造は単体では成立していません。上部にある水平のH型鋼がラメラドームと繋がれていて、一体の構造になっています。単体のドームだと座屈しやすく、しかもジョイントがピンで安定しないので、上の屋根と一体になって成立しているんです。ドームなのだけれど屋根はフラットで、ドームで屋根の荷重を支えているのですが、局所的な変形や座屈等が起きないようにしているのは屋根の梁なんです。おそらく施工の時も、下のドームだけだと安定しないという状況だったと思います。

仙田　ドームの部分は建築的に塔屋の部分であって、全体の8分の1の部分が上がっている。だから建築法規ギリギリでやっているわけです（笑）。また、そこからハイサイドライトを得ているという、絶妙な感じで成り立っているところなんだ。あそこから光が入ってこなければ、全く別の感じになっていると思う。

repeating uniform grid, whereas an ellipse has a different form and size for each part of the dome, which leads to the amusing look.

There were two main reasons for the overall delicate feel: one was because we clang to the dome shape and made the most out of it, and one was because we did away with horizontal members like hoops.

Senda: The roof for the "Great Hall," as it's called, was a great success, as it lets you view seventy thousand books in one sight. The delicate structure of the space, together with the blue paint which is a reference to Seisonkaku, a shoin-style building once used by the Maeda family, bring great effects to the space.

Kanebako: Yes, the contrast between the color of the dome and the blue on the upper part is striking.

To supplement what I told about the structure, this delicate dome does not hold on its own. The horizontal H-beams above are connected to the lamella dome, to form an integrated structure. Since the dome in itself is easy to buckle, and unstable due to the pin joints, it needs to be unified with the roof above it to hold its shape. It is a dome but with a flat roof, whose load is supported by the dome, while the beams protect against local deformations and bucklings. I believe the dome couldn't stay stable alone during construction.

Senda: The dome is the penthouse part of the whole building, with one eighth of the total footprint raised, which is barely within the legal limit (laughs). But it magically provides light from the high-side windows. Otherwise, the space could have felt totally different.

少しずつ形も大きさも異なるグリッド
楕円ならではの視覚的な魅力がある（金箱）

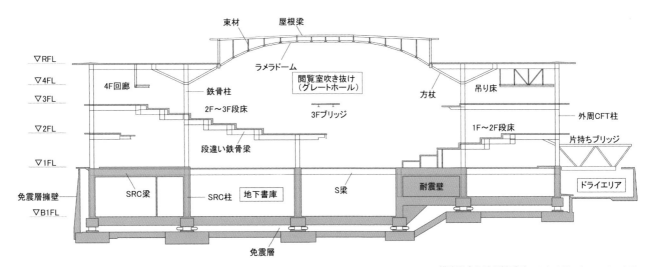

構造形式を示す断面図。ラメラドームのスラストは柱の内側と外側の方杖材を介して周囲のRCスラブに伝えられ、スラブのリング状の効果で抵抗させている。2、3階の段床部では段差梁が用いられており、最下層に免震層が設けられている（金箱）

図中ラベル：
▽RFL ▽4FL ▽3FL ▽2FL ▽1FL ▽B1FL
束材　屋根梁　ラメラドーム　閲覧室吹き抜け（グレートホール）　方杖　吊り床
4F回廊　鉄骨柱　2F～3F段床　3Fブリッジ　外周CFT柱
段違い鉄骨梁　1F～2F段床　片持ちブリッジ
免震層擁壁　SRC梁　SRC柱　地下書庫　S梁　耐震壁　ドライエリア
免震層

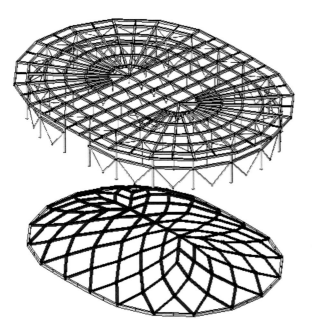

屋根架構のアクソメ図。上段のフラットな屋根構造と下段のラメラドームが束材で一体化されている。一体化することでラメラドームの座屈強度が高められている（金箱）

ドームの鉄骨詳細図。束材に厚肉の鋼管を用いてガセットプレートを部材角度に合わせて溶接。ラチス部材は、アングルを角が外側となるように組み合わせて使用し、端部で内側に取りつけたプレートとガセットプレートに高力ボルトで留めている（金箱）

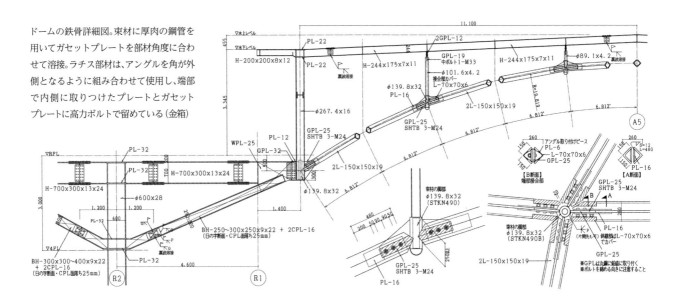

特徴的な形状の部材と超高難度の施工
Specially Designed Members and Extremely Challenging Construction

金箱　また、ドームの部材の形状はかなり特徴的だと思います。ただ、あの部材をいったい、いつ決めたのかというのが、あまり記憶がないんですよ（笑）。仙田先生といろいろやりとりをしていた際に、あまり部材のイメージはなかったのですが、ある時に角形になっていたのを覚えています。でも、角形鋼管をそのまま使うと、端部のディテールがすごく難しいんですよね。

それでどうしようかと言っているうちに、アングルを二つ組み合わせて中にプレートを仕込んで、ボルトで留めよう。ボルトを留めるためにアングルの端部を欠き込んでおいて、最後に現場で溶接するという話なのですが、その肝心のところは僕ではなく、担当者が関与して決まったのだと思います（笑）

でき上がった建物を見た方から、あれは木造ですか？と言われたんです。色のせいもありますが、エッジが効いているからですね。僕は京都駅で角形鋼管を使ったのですが、エッジが丸いんですね。ああいう色でボルトが中に仕込まれた木造みたいな形状になっているというのがポイントですね。

仙田　環境デザイン研究所(E.D.I.)のビルのプレートとか、手すりやサインなど、角パイプを45度傾けるのは、私がよく使っている手法なんだよね。

金箱　昔、常滑の体育館などでも使われていましたね。

仙田　そういった経験もあって、また、下から見た時に少しシャープにしたいということもあって角材を振るということを提案したのですが、アングルを合わせるというのが、非常によい解決だったと思いますね。

Kanebako: The dome members themselves have pretty unique profiles. But I don't really remember when exactly we decided on that particular shape (laughs). What I remember is, in our early discussions with Mr. Senda, we didn't talk much about the members, but at some point, a box profile rose to the surface. The problem was, if you simply used box steel tubes, the details at the ends would be very difficult.

Later in the discussion, we came up with the idea of coupling two angles with plates inside and using bolts on the plates. The end tips of the angles were cut off to make space for working on the bolts and would be welded up on-site. One of my staff was involved in the essential part of these details, not me, unfortunately (laughs).

Someone saw the completed building and asked me if it was wooden. I reckon it was not just because of the color, but the sharp edges. I used box tubes for the Kyoto Station building, but those had round edges. Here, the point is the combination of the color and the wooden-like shape that hides bolts inside.

Senda: Rotating box pipes by 45 degrees is a familiar technique for me, as I have used it for the nameplate of my Environment Design Institute building, or for handrails and signs.

Kanebako: You also used it for the gymnasium in Tokoname.

Senda: Because I had such experiences, and because I wanted to make them look a bit sharp from below, I suggested rotating the pipes for the dome members, and in the end, coupling two angles turned out to be a great solution.

2、3階の南側グレートホール開架書架部分の鉄骨架構状況。階高を詰め、床段差に対応するよう放射状に架構されたスラブ受け段型梁は製作、建方ともに難易度が高かった。この後、鉄筋コンクリートで仕上げに合わせた段型、スロープの床を構築した（亀井・金箱）

屋根鉄骨の建方状況。フラットな屋根鉄骨架構とラメラドームの斜材を束材で一体化している。束材に取り合う斜材は3次元で架構され、長さ、方向が一本ずつ違うため、人力で取りつけた。束材と斜材の節点は切り欠いてボルト留めの後、同材のアングルで塞いだ（亀井・金箱）

非常に難度の高い工事であり
全社的な支援を受けて進めました（亀井）

亀井　そうですね。やはりグレートホールのドームのトラス、それがこの建物の一番の見どころだと思います。ドームの鉄骨の架構というのは難度の高い工事なのですが、その他の鉄骨架構も非常に難度の高いものでした。特に円形で段状となっている部分です。この部分が仕上げ材で隠れてしまっているのは非常に残念です。

具体的に言うと柱についての話になるのですが、我々が普通に考えると1階から同じ位置に柱があるはずなのですが、この建物は途中階の2階や3階から柱が発生するんです（笑）。それは意匠的に必要な空間を確保するという考えで設計されたということなのですが、実際に施工する側にとっては、やはり手ごわいですよね。それを組み上げていって、最終的に成立するというような架構ですので。

現場で一本一本組み上げていくには支保工が必要で、その支保工を解放するのはいつがいいのかという問題もありました。鉄骨組立後のスラブコンクリート打設があり、その荷重がかかった時がいいのか、はたまた前がいいのか。そのあたりも検証させていただきました。

私もこれだけ難易度の高い鉄骨の架構をやらせてもらったのは初めてです。当社が受注した際も、超高難度の建物なので、全社的な対応で進めるということでスタートし、社内的な支援を受けながら、何とかうまく進めることができたと思っています。

また、天井面ドームの斜材接合部の仕上げ処理には結構手間がかかりました。ボルトを処理した後、切り欠き部に同材のアングルのキャップ

Kamei: I agree. The trusses of the Great Hall dome is the highlight of the building. Building steelworks for the dome itself was difficult, but frameworks for the other parts were also extremely challenging, especially the circular steps. It is unfortunate that we cannot see these parts now, as they are hidden by the finishes.

Specifically, an ordinary design has columns at the same positions on every floor, extending from the first floor and up, whereas this building has columns that start from the second or third floors (laughs). This was an intentional design to secure necessary spaces from architectural points of view, but was difficult for us builders nevertheless. It was a type of structure that only held shape when everything was finally in place.

It needed supports while it was being built one element by one, so we had to think about when to remove those supports. After the steel framework was installed, concrete slabs were supposed to be cast on top, so we confirmed a better timing to remove the supports—before or after the load of the slabs was placed.

For me, it was the most challenging steel framework I had ever experienced. It was such an extremely difficult project that, when our company received the order, the whole company was involved from the start, and we managed to proceed with help from inside.

The finishing of the dome member joints was also a time-consuming process. It took so many hours to treat the bolts, fill the cutoff hole of the angles with the same material, seam-weld, grind, and finally paint them.

をあてて、全溶接後に平滑処理をして、最終的に塗装仕上げすると
いうのは、やはり時間を要しました。2次元であれば下で地組みを
したものを、大型クレーンで持ち上げて組むということも考えられるの
ですが、ここの3次元の架構では、それはできなかったので、一本一本
の部材を人の手で足場をつくって、その上で組み立てていったんです。
そのための足場を下から組み立てるわけですが、それを使って最終
的な塗装仕上げや電気・設備の器具付けを順番に行っていくわけで
すが、下から足場が立っていると下部の作業ができません。今回は
下部に段状の鉄骨の梁があって、その上でRCでスラブなり階段なり
をつくっていくという手間のかかる仕事があって、それが、なかなか
できないという問題があったのですが、最近は結構便利な仮設材が
ありまして。屋根のG梁から吊り足場を吊る「クイックデッキ」と
いうものですが、フラットで隙間のない床がつくれて、その上でいわ
ゆる立ち馬等が使用できるんですね。
今回はそれを天井仕上げのルーバー取付レベルで組んで、1層目の
仕事は立ち馬を使ってやる。2層目もまた低い立ち馬を使って、最終
的に天井のルーバーの仕上げを吊り足場の盛り替えなしで行いました。
こういったかたちで上下同時作業を可能にし、下の段状の仕上げも
並行して進めることができたので、それは非常にうまくいったのでは
ないかと思います。

A two-dimensional structure could have been constructed on the ground and lifted by a large crane, but for this three-dimensional structure, we had to work on each element on a manually erected scaffolding.

The scaffolding was erected from the ground and was used in turn for painting finishes and installing electricity or other equipment, but it would also prohibit working on the lower levels. Especially in this project, we had the stepped steel beams below, and we had to take time to build concrete slabs and stairs on top of them, which would have been deterred by the scaffolding. Luckily, we found a handy type of scaffolds called "Quick Decks," which provided flat and seamless platforms suspended from the roof girders and allowed using horse scaffolds on them.

In this case, we used these decks at the stage where we installed the louver ceilings, using horse scaffolds for the first layer, and using lower ones for the second layer, and eventually completed all the louver finishes without reinstalling the decks. This way we made it possible to work on the upper and lower parts of the building at the same time, so that we could proceed on the finishes on the steps in the lower part while other parts were still being worked on. In the end this was a great success.

本をめくるイメージを支える外壁の「下地」

Substrates Were Keys to Flipped Book Effect on Exterior Walls

仙田　もう一つ、ここの図書館の特徴として大きいのは外壁のパネル
ですね。本をめくるというイメージで、平面的に四角の部分がめく
れ上がっているように見せているわけです。エレベーションの案を
いくつもつくって、モックアップもつくっていただきましたが、施工
上の難しさも相当あったと思います。
亀井　外壁パネルは2種類、フラットパネルと3次元曲面のパネル
があったのですが、フラットパネルの設計図を最初に見て、ちょっと
現実的な下地としては難しいかな、ということがありました。ここ
は意匠上、袖壁が60cm、支点から跳ね出しというか持ち出している
んですね。設計図では平面のタイル下地が穴あきPC板になってい
たのですが、それがメーカーの許容値をオーバーしていたんですね。
下がり壁の方も同じく60cm支点から跳ね出しているのですが、許容
値オーバーで対応できないということがあったんです。10cmの穴
あきPC板の小口に軽量鉄骨で、はしご状の鉄骨をくっつけて下地
とするというような設計図だったのですが、実際にこれをやろうと
した場合、うちの技術部曰く、すっきりしたものにはならないよ、

Senda: Another compelling feature of this library is the exterior wall panels. We made them look like rectangular planes being flipped at their edges, so that they capture the way we flip through pages of a book. We went through countless elevation studies, along with a mockup thanks to the builders, and I also believe the actual construction was quite as difficult.

Kamei: There were two types of exterior wall panels: the flat ones and the ones with three-dimensional curves. When I first saw the flat panel drawings, I thought the substrates would be impractical. These parts had 60-centimeter cantilevered wing walls, which were above the manufacturer's allowable tolerance for the voided precast panels specified on the drawings as the backing behind the tiles. Especially, where these 60-centimeter cantilevers extended to the hanging parts of the panels, they could not be supported due to tolerance issues. The drawing said there was a lightweight steel ladder-frame attached to the profile of the 10-centimeter-thick voided concrete panels, but if we were to build it in reality, our technology team told it was not going to be

ということでした。

どういうことかというと、基本的に風圧など、いろいろな外力が働いた時に、接続部が強度的に弱いので、それを担保するための別の補強材が必要ということでした。そこで金箱事務所の望月（泰宏）さんにもご相談して、2、3階のスラブの先端にRCで梁状に受けをつくって、その上にパネルを乗せるというかたちにして、RCの受けをそのまま跳ね出し、持ち出し部分まで延長して、その上にパネルをそのまま乗せられるというかたちにしました。厚みもパネルと同じ幅にさせてもらって、これなら間違いないということで、相談しながら変更をさせていただきました。ここは意匠上、外壁として見えるところで数もありますし、将来何十年も残さなければなりませんから、強度的にも安心できるものになったのではないかと思います。

それとめくれあがっている部分、3次元曲面の仕上がりについて。これも下地についてですが、図面を最初見た時に、板金の屋根を縦使いにして、縦ハゼ葺きの屋根の板金に対して特殊な金具で挟み込んで下地＋タイルの重量を支持するという、そういう納まりだったのですが、重量的に800～900kgあったので、その挟み込みで本当

that slender.

Specifically, the joints were too weak against wind and other external forces, and needed additional reinforcements. We consulted Mr. Yasuhiro Mochizuki from Kanebako Structural Engineers, and decided to attach supporting RC beams to the edges of the second and third floor slabs, extend the supports to the cantilevered parts, and place the panels on them. We made the supports in the same thickness as the panels, and talked to the designers and engineers to make sure everything was going to work perfectly, before making final changes. Since these exterior walls would be architectural features of the building and there were numbers of them, we took extra cares to guarantee their strength to make them last for several decades.

There were other challenges with the three-dimensional curves in the flipped panels, again with their substrates. On the drawing, a standing seam metal roofing was clamped by a special type of attachment parts to support the furrings and the tiles, and we were unsure if the clamping mechanism was strong enough to support that hefty 800 to 900 kilograms.

We asked for advice for these parts as well, and decided to make precise

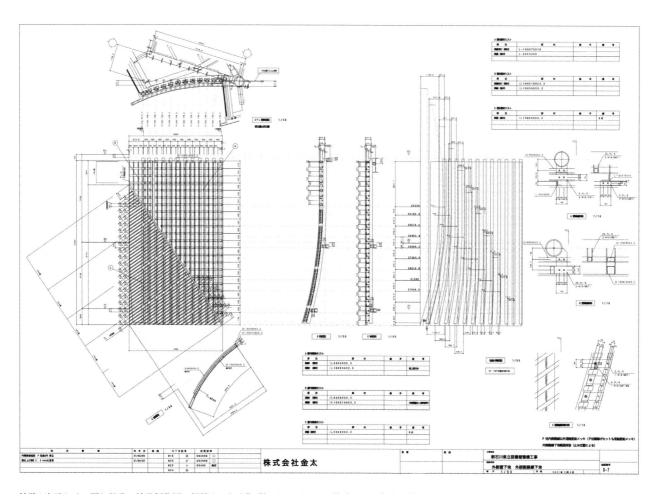

外壁3次元タイル張り部分の鉄骨製作図。鋼管を3次元曲げ加工し、G-PLで外壁タイル荷重を支持している。ページをめくるような柔らかな曲線を実現するため、柱一本ごとにRの加工が異なっている。袖壁の跳ね出し部分は決められた薄さを確保するため、柱に取りつく下地材をユニットで一体化し、跳ね出すこととしたものを工場製作して現場で取りつけた。結果、強度も仕上げの出来栄えも設計の意図通りのものとなった（亀井）

に大丈夫か、という話がありました。

これについてもご相談させてもらって、3次元曲面をきれいに出すためには、やっぱり下地からきちっとした曲面が出せると仕上げが容易になるので、それに沿って張っていこうと。当初、下地を角柱で見てもらっていたのですが、3次元曲面に曲加工するために鋼管に変えさせてもらいました。また、その厚みなども再度検討していただいて、強度的に大丈夫というところを再確認していただきました。その柱からの持ち出しで十分な強度のあるガセットで、鉄骨の胴縁と3次元曲面に合わせたものを工場で加工し、組み立てたものを現場に搬入して、そのままボルト取りしました。それで3次元の面を確保し、いわゆる止水ラインの板金処理も施しました。

あとはタイル仕上げ面が外壁止水ラインから10cmほど持ち出しているのですが、そこのタイルのバックにもう一度板金を設えました。ダブルスキンとすることで、漏水対策も十分になるということでやらせてもらいました。

こういったかたちで外壁についてはフラット面も3次元の面も、下地について自信を持っておわたしできることになったと思いますし、設計通りの、きれいな曲面で仕上がったのかなと思います。

仙田　それは非常に感謝しています。当初、発泡コンクリートで全てのパネルをつくろうという案もありましたが、そうするとメーカーはかなり大変だという話がありましたね。最終的にフラットな部分と、めくれ上がった部分を異なる部材で構成することによって、全体の形態がうまくでき上がったということですね。

curves at the framework level and use them as guidelines for the finishes. In the initial design, the vertical frames were square tubes, but in order to warp them into three-dimensional surfaces, we had them changed to round tubes. We also asked to revise the thickness of the tubes to ensure their strength. We used those tubes as pillars to attach solid gusset plates that supported steel furrings, all aligned with the three-dimensional curves, assembled them at the plant, and brought into the site to bolt them to the main structure. This way we created the three-dimensional surface and formed the water shield layer covered with metal roofing. Additionally, we installed another metal roofing layer on the back of the tiles, whose outer surface was separated from the water shield layer by about ten centimeters. We wanted to be extra sure about containing leakage by creating a double-skin roof.

We are confident about the resulting outer wall substrates, both for the flat panels and the curved ones, and we are pleased to have recreated the beautiful curves from the drawings.

Senda: I really appreciate all your effort there. At early stages we were talking about creating all the panels with aerated concrete, but it turned out to be too difficult for the manufacturers. In the end, using different materials for the flat and the flipped panels resulted in the overall integrity.

限られた高さの中に、いかに空間や機能を盛り込むか

Incorporating Spaces and Functions in a Limited Height

金箱　先ほどお話ししたグリッドや段差についてですが、高さが限られている中で計画的に必要な空間を詰めるという意味で工夫が必要でした。施工中の写真を見るとよくわかるのですが、段差上に鉄骨の梁が放射状に配置されるという、特殊なかたちになりました。全体的にかなり複雑な架構なのですが、図書館としての機能性維持のために、免震を採用していることの効果が大きいですね。複雑な構造をそれほど無理なく成立させていると思います。

図書館で免震構造を採用している事例はあまりないと思うのですが、前に手がけた埼玉の図書館では東日本大震災の際、建物自体には全く損傷がなかったけれど、本が棚から落ちて、整理が大変だったという話を聞いたことがあります。図書館の免震というのは、安全性はもちろんなのですが、継続的に施設を使うことができるという意味

Kanebako: Speaking about the column grid layouts and the steps I mentioned earlier, arranging necessary spaces in these height-limited conditions required some effort. As you can see in the construction photograph, we placed stepped steel beams in radial arrangements, which was very unusual as a composition. As a whole, the structure of the building is quite complicated, but it was mainly thanks to the use of seismic isolation that made it possible in a largely straightforward way.

As far as I know, only a few library buildings use seismic isolation structure, but what I was told about one of my past works—a library in Saitama—was that despite the building itself remaining totally intact during the Great East Japan Earthquake, they still had to sort out through all the books that fell off the shelves. As much as being a safety measure, isolation for libraries is also beneficial to the building's service continuity.

でメリットが大きいと思うんです。

ただ、閲覧室は無柱の空間なので、免震化に際しては結構難しいことがありました。免震といえども、主体構造はある程度の剛性を持たなければならないので、ここでは1階の柱をダブルにして、途中に梁を繋いだり、中にコンクリートを詰めたり、考えられることは全て組み込みました。下のグリッドが異なって段差があるということを、どのように解決するのか、しかもそれを免震構造として全体をいかに成立させるかが、下部の構造のテーマでした。

仙田　今回は設計者として模型をつくって確認したつもりでしたが、納まり的にわからないところがありました。現場でこんな風になるんだと理解することが多々ありましたね。それほど、直交の軸と円形の段床との交点の様々な納まりを検討せざるを得ませんでした。

これからつくられる県立規模の図書館でも、免震構造はしっかり取り組まれると思うのですが、ここでは、いわゆる柱頭免震ではなくて、下からドサッと、書架を丸ごと扱っているから、地下工事も結構大変だったと思うのですが、トラブルはありませんでしたか。

亀井　トラブルは特になかったですね。杭や水についてもなかったです。

仙田　やっぱり、丘の上につくるという利点があったと思いますね。

金箱　この建物は、断面図を見て振り返ってみると高さとの闘いでしたね。

仙田　そう、高さの中にいかに機能を盛り込むかというね。

金箱　だから床は段状の梁でつくらざるを得なかったんですよね。

仙田　4階の回廊も上から吊っています。あれが4階を成立させていて、ここの図書館に新しい視線、視点をもたらしていると思っているんだけどね。

免震以外にも、私はこれまでこどもの施設を手がけてきたから、安全面について、あちこち気を使ったところがありました。例えば最上階ではガラスの手すりを1m800まで上げて、端の方は1m300に

However, because the reading areas were open spaces without pillars, in order to apply the isolation, some tough adjustments had to be made. Seismic isolation still required a certain level of rigidity to the main structure, which led us to incorporate every possible measure from doubling some of the first-floor columns with girders in between, to filling the steel columns with concrete. How to solve problems of having steps with different grid layouts below, and how to integrate everything into a single isolated structure were the main themes for the lower structure.

Senda: Although we had scrutinized every detail in scale models, they still left some parts unsolved even for us designers, until we finally figured them out on-site. There were so many variations to consider for the details where the grid layout intersected with the circular steps.

I think seismic isolation will also be used in future prefectural-level libraries, but in our case, we did not place the isolators on top of the columns, but below the foundation to support the whole archive, which I imagine must have added to groundwork difficulties. Have you encountered any trouble?

Kamei: Not particularly, to be honest. There were no problems with the piles or groundwater either.

Senda: Looks like the hilltop location worked favorably.

Kanebako: Looking back at the section drawings, this project was full of challenges with height limitations.

Senda: Exactly. It was all about how to incorporate functions within the limited height.

Kanebako: That was why we had to build the floors with stepped beams.

Senda: The Ring Aisle on the fourth floor is suspended from above for the same reason. This part is what gives the fourth floor meaning and provides a new viewpoint to this library.

Aside from seismic isolation, I also took extra care of safety in many

するなど、結構配慮しました。

それから真ん中のブリッジのところは少し揺れるんだよね。一本柱でどうしても揺れるのだけれど、特にクレームはないようですね。

金箱　そうですね。あそこは椅子が置かれていて、座っていると振動を感じるんですよね。ブリッジや階段は普通、建築家は繊細につくりたいものだと思います。でも、でき上がったものがガッチリしていると、ガッチリし過ぎとか言われるし（笑）。ほどよく揺れるぐらいがちょうどいいのかもしれません。

仙田　あのくらいの揺れはいいんじゃないかな。「めまいの空間」なんて呼んでいるわけだからね（笑）

金箱　おそらく椅子に座っていなければ、全然気がつかないと思うんです。

仙田　こどもエリアにも、揺れを楽しむチューブ状のネット遊具があるからね。

余談ですが、こどもエリアは段状のスラブの下にありますが、私はあそこに穴を開けようと画策したんですよ（笑）。こどもエリアから大空間を覗く穴をつくったり、地下の書架を覗き見る穴をつくったりという計画をしていたのだけれど、皆さんの反対もあって実現できなかったのです。

parts, as I had been designing buildings for children in the past. For example, I raised the height of the glass fence on the uppermost floor to 1.8 meters, leaving 1.3 meter part at the ends.

The Bridge in the middle wobbles a bit, because it is supported on a single row of posts. However, we haven't had any complaints about it, have we?

Kanebako: No, we haven't. When we sit on one of the chairs there, we feel the wobble. It is usual for architects to prefer delicate designs for bridges and staircases, and they tend to complain about the result being too sturdy (laughs). A bit of shakiness might be just the right balance for it.

Senda: Yes, I think that amount of wobble is fairly acceptable, especially as we call it the "place for dizziness" (laughs).

Kanebako: We wouldn't notice unless we sit in the chairs.

Senda: We even have a playset for children to enjoy swinging around in a tube net, in the Children's Area.

Speaking of which, I had a plot to punch holes through the stepped slab, where Children's Area is located right below (laughs). I was thinking of making peepholes from the Children's Area to the Great Hall, or through to the underground archives, which everyone opposed and I eventually had to give up.

素材と共に、館内全体の色彩にも配慮
Considerations on Materials and Overall Color Scheme

仙田　内装については、石川県から地元木材の利用についてリクエストされたのですが、素材の調達など、ご苦労はありませんでしたか。

亀井　そうですね。結構ボリュームのある天井ルーバーが1〜3階に設けられているのですが、元々は石川県産の能登ヒバを使用する設計でした。能登ヒバは石川県でも限られた地域でしか産出しない貴重なもので、不燃処理したものがあちこちで使われているようで、なかなかよい材料を確保するのが難しい状況でした。そこで、県産のスギであれば生産量も多く、まとまった量を確保できるということで併せてご提案しました。最終的には能登ヒバは家具や書架などに使用して、天井ルーバーには県産のスギを使わせていただきました。

仙田　書架や天井ルーバーなど、素材だけでなく、色彩も全体的に調整していただいて、うまく納めていただいたのではないかと思います。

亀井　ルーバーは1、2階は100×15でフラットで張ってあります。3階の天井は縦の吹き寄せの放射状で、かなりボリュームもありました。ぱっと見はそんなに難しく見えないかもしれませんが、吹抜けにかかっている部分もありましたし、後で歪んできた、みたいなことがあると大変ですので、やはり社内で検討を重ねて取り組みました。

Senda: As for the interior materials, we had a request from Ishikawa Prefecture about using local wood. Were there any difficulties concerning supply of those materials?

Kamei: From the first through the third floors, we had fair numbers of louver ceilings which was originally specified in the drawings as local Noto cypress, a rare type of wood only produced in a limited area in the prefecture. Fireproofed lumber from this wood was used in numerous other projects, and it was difficult for us to secure our amount of good quality supply of this material. Instead, we proposed an option of using local cedar, which was abundant in production and easily available in quantities. In the end, we decided to use Noto cypress for furniture and shelves, while using local cedar for louver ceilings.

Senda: I appreciate your effort in managing those materials for the shelves and the louvers, as well as the overall color scheme, which came out greatly satisfying.

Kamei: The louver elements on the first and the second floors had a profile of 100 by 15 millimeters, laid out on their wider faces. The ones on the third floor were greater in numbers, and they were laid out radially, using elements upright in groups. They didn't seem complicated by the looks, but because some parts of them were hanging above the large void, which would be a problem in case of later deformation and

ボリュームがありましたので、それをきちっと通りよく、歪み防止も考慮して、工場でユニット化しました。スリット天井となっている天井内部は全て黒く塗装してあるのですが、縦ルーバーを繋いで固定する木の不燃材を黒く塗装して目立たないようにして、600幅×4m長のユニットとして組んだものを現場に持ち込んで、そのまま天井の下地に固定しました。結果的によい精度で、安全に施工できたものと思います。

仙田　おかげさまで県の皆さんのご要望に応える仕上がりになりました。ありがとうございました。

2023年3月30日収録

other flaws, we made careful studies before deciding on the final shape. In order to align large numbers of them perfectly and to prevent deformation, we decided to preassemble them in modules. We connected the upright louver elements with fireproofed wood parts and painted those parts black to camouflage them against the blacked-out background of the ceiling, assembled them into 600-millimeter-by-4-meter modules, brought them into the site and fixed them on the ceiling framework. As a result, we managed to realize a high level of precision in a safe construction method.

Senda: Thanks to all your efforts, I am confident that the finished building meets the expectations of the citizens of Ishikawa. I really appreciate it.

Interviewed on March 30, 2023

3、4階の階段踊り場にて、眼下のグレートホール開架書架を見る。コロシアムのように円形段状に配置された7万冊の書架が一望でき、東西を繋ぐ3階のブリッジと間近に見える天井ラメラドームの迫力が際立つ、今までにない図書館となった（亀井）

約40×50mの大空間を支えるラメラドーム。トップサイドからの光が
グレートホールを柔らかく満たす。天井の青色は前田家成巽閣の群青
の間から発想したもの。

アングルの角が外側となるように組み合わせ、端部で局所的に内側に取りつけたプレートで両側の部材をガセットプレートに挟み込み、ボルト留めとしたディテール。構造合理性とデザイン性、施工性を追求している。

トップサイドからの柔らかい光に包まれるグレートホールを一望する。

4階のリングより、2階と3階を繋ぐ半円形の段状書架を見る。

乾式工法でつくられた50角のタイルと鉄骨による外壁パネル。
本をめくるイメージを具現化している。

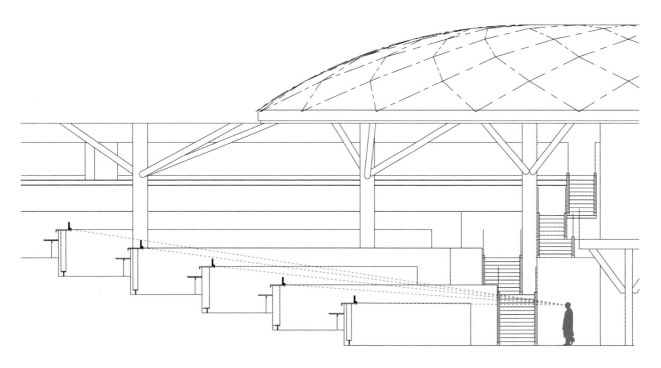

エントランスを抜け
グレートホールに入ると
空間がパッと広がり心が躍る!!
その瞬間が素晴らしい。

　　　廣村正彰

II
Signs and Lighting

公園のようにめぐり、本と触れ合う喜びを享受する空間とは？

What is a space where one can find joy in reading while exploring like a park?

面出 薫
Kaoru MENDE

ライティング プランナーズ
アソシエーツ代表

×

廣村正彰
Masaaki HIROMURA

廣村デザイン事務所代表

×

仙田 満
Mitsuru SENDA

環境デザイン研究所会長

サインと照明。いずれも公共施設において重要な役割を果たしているが、
両者の連関について考える機会はなかなかないのではないだろうか。
仙田氏曰く、これらが石川県立図書館の居心地のよさを生み出しているのだという。
スペシャリスト三人による建築空間デザイン論に耳を傾けてみよう。

Signs and lighting—it is not often that we examine the relationship between the two,
despite their valuable contribution in public facilities.
In fact, however, they play major roles in creating comfort in the Ishikawa Prefectural Library, according to Mr. Senda.
This issue delves deeply into the architectural space design theories of three specialists.

驚きつつ、動き回る
Wandering around with Surprises

仙田　最近、創造には「集中」と「ワンダリング」が必要だと考えているのですが、この建物では光とサインのデザインが、それぞれに非常に大きな役割を果たしていると思います。まさに図書館内を「歩き回る」きっかけを与えてくれているわけです。

廣村　はじめにこの図書館の企画資料を見せていただいた時、「めぐる、めくる、めくるめく」と書かれていたのですが、一つのワードとしてよくできていて、仙田先生が提唱している「遊環構造空間」を体現していますよね。それがいいなと思ったんです。

僕は、ここの図書館には二つのテーマ、狙いがあるのではないかと考えていました。一つは「感動体験」をつくり出すということ。もう一つは「快適時間」。ここで過ごしていても、飽きないんですよね。

仙田　居続けられるというかね。

廣村　それを言うのは簡単だけれど、実際には大変なことですよね。快適な時間が過ぎていくということを実現すること。それに対して我々がデザインを通じてできることを、しっかりとやっていきたいというのが最初の思いです。

面出　仙田さんの「集中」と「ワンダリング」に関連して言うと、照明の世界でも高品質な「ワオ」や「驚き」ということを考えます。いつもと違ったものが感じられたり、新たな自分を発見したり、といったことですね。

ただ驚かせるだけの照明はたくさんあるわけですが、品質がよくないと下品になってしまう。そうではなくて、「ああ、これは違うな」と感じるような高品質なワンダリングというものが明らかにあるんです。今日も雪の中を歩いてきて、図書館に入ったところで「うわっ」と言っている人を見ましたよ。最初にパッとこの空間に囲まれた時の「驚き」ですよね。

この図書館に入ってくる人々は仙田さんの設計の"罠"にはまって、驚きつつ、動き回っている。そして回遊する人々に対応する景色をうまくつくることができたのではないかと思います。自然光と人工光のバランスをこれだけ上手にとることができた空間はなかなかないのではないでしょうか。

廣村　エントランスとグレートホールがダブルDで互い違いになっているというのは、建築の企てとして魅力的です。エントランスからホールに入っていくと、急に視界が開けて、皆、あーって見上げるんですよね（笑）。天井からは光が降り注いでいて、開放感と共に壮大な空間がそこにあるという。そういう光景を目の当たりにすると、これはサインを逐一見て理解するよりも、実際に館内をめぐっていけば自然にわかるのでは、と思いました。

サインは「驚きつつ、動き回る」を助ける役割を果たしているわけですが、この取り組みのベースには司書の方々の編集能力の高さがあり、それはこの図書館の魅力の一つとなっている。ずらりと並べ

Senda: I've been thinking lately that "concentration" and "wandering" are imperative for creation, and lighting and signs go a long way toward encouraging people to wander around this library.

Hiromura: I was very intrigued that the single phrase "Explore, Encounter, Experience" written in the project materials perfectly embodies your concept of the "circular play system theory."

I was assuming that there are two underlying themes and objectives for this library: one is to create an emotional experience, and the other is to create a comfortable time. In fact, you never get bored in this place.

Senda: It's like you can stay here forever.

Hiromura: Easier said than done, but in reality, it surely requires a lot of work to make these things happen. We have always been committed to the pursuit of comfort through design.

Mende: The concentration and wandering that Mr. Senda mentioned can be replaced with high-quality "wows" and "surprises" in the lighting world; an encounter with something extraordinary or a discovery of new selves.

There are plenty of lights that simply surprise you, but it would be just vulgar lighting if it lacked good quality. There is clearly a high-quality wandering that you can sensibly recognize as something different. In fact, I just came across a person walking to the library today in the snow, who literally said "Wow" as he stepped in. That is the kind of surprise you get when you are in this space for the first time.

Visitors to this library are all caught in Mr. Senda's "design trap" to wander around with surprises. And we have created such perfect views that amaze them. Very few spaces are able to achieve such a good balance between natural and artificial light.

Hiromura: One of the most intriguing architectural schemes in this building is the entrance and the Great Hall, which are alternately arranged with double D. The view that suddenly opens up as one enters the hall from the entrance naturally leads people's eyes to the ceiling (laughs). As I stood in a space filled with openness and grandeur, with light pouring down from the ceiling, I couldn't help but wonder if the visitors would spontaneously reach their destinations as they actually wander around the library, rather than being guided by a sign.

Behind the creation of the signs that allow people to wander around with surprises lies the high editorial skills of the librarians, which is also part of the charm of this library. It is hard not to get excited as you look at the covers lined up on the bookshelves. Time passes quickly as I pick up books that interest me.

While there are other circular libraries built in the past, the circular slope arrangement makes this library particularly unique, which makes for a very impactful view. In sign design, we designed a series of typefaces and put them above the bookshelves to make them readable from a distance and attract people's interest.

【自分を表現する】EXPRESSING YOURSELF　　　【身体を動かす】MOVING YOUR BODY

【世界に飛び出す】DISCOVERING THE WORLD　　【好奇心を抱く】BEING CURIOUS　　【生き方に学ぶ】LEARNING FROM DIFFERENT LIVES

【日本を知る】GETTING TO KNOW JAPAN　　【仕事を考える】THINKING ABOUT WORK

【暮らしを広げる】BROADENING YOUR LIFESTYLE　　【文学にふれる】EXPERIENCING LITERATURE

本との出会いの窓　　【里の恵み・文化の香り〜石川コレクション〜】

グレートホール内、配架のテーマを示すサインの概念図（廣村）

られた表紙を眺めていくと、興味が湧いてきてしょうがないんです
よね。これ読んでみたい、これ見てみたいと、それだけで時間が過ぎ
ていってしまうという感じです。
これまでも円形の図書館はつくられてきたのですが、ここはスロー
プで回遊していくんですよね。それがビューとしての見どころに
なっているわけですが、サインについては興味を惹くように、遠く
からでも配架のテーマが認識できた方がよいのではないかと考え、
活字書体の文字が、書架の上に並ぶかたちとしました。
それがどうしたら見やすく、わかりやすくなるだろうかと考えて、
ああこれは照明だと。面出さんに書架の上に立てるサインにうまく
照明が当たるようにできないか、効果的な照明の方法はないだろう
かと相談したんです。
試行錯誤して、グレートホールの濃い茶色のしっとりとした空間の
中に、白い文字が浮かび上がるというサインができたわけです。
面出　サインの言葉の意味も「世界に飛び出す」とか、様々な編集
が施されていて、キャッチーでいいですよね。

When we were developing a strategy to make those signs stand out,
it occurred to me that lighting could be the key. I consulted with Mr.
Mende about the way to effectively illuminate the signs above the
bookshelves.

At long last, the signs were completed with white lettering that
contrasted with the elegant dark brown of the Great Hall.

Mende: I like the fact that the wordings of each sign are edited to be so
eye-catching, such as "Dive into the World."

自然光の魅力と難しさ

The Magic and Complexity of Natural Light

面出　仙田さんとはいろいろな建物で一緒にお仕事をしていますが、ここの建物を見た時になるほどと思いました。我々は「作業の光」と「周辺の光」を「タスク＆アンビエント」と言うのですが、この図書館では全体を照らすのではなくて、必要な部分に美しい陰影があるんです。作業に必要な作業面の光、ファンクションとしての光を与えて、あとは景色をつくるための、建築を活かすためのアンビエントな光を整えていく。仙田さんの図書館建築は、大空間の中で、それらを見事に実現していると思います。

ファンクションだけでは図書館は機能しません。廣村さんが言ったように快適であるということが必要で、何を快適と感じるかがカギになります。ここではデイライト（昼光）を取り入れているのですが、ベンガラ色や木の暖かい色味となかなかうまい具合に共存していますよね。

仙田　昼光とおっしゃいましたが、私は外からの光がないとすごく不安なんです。閉鎖的な空間がダメで、空とか外が見えないと嫌なんですよ。そういう昼光があって、手元に基本的な光があるというのが望ましい。

面出　建築家は仙田さんだけでなく、だいたい昼光に対する憧れがありますよね。ルイス・カーンにも『Light is the Theme』という光が主題になった、キンベルアートミュージアムの小冊子があるのですが、人工の照明には一切触れていないんですよ。自然の光がどうやって入ってくるか、ということだけに気を使っているんです。

建築家というのはアーティフィシャル（人工的）な空間というのはあまり

Mende: Of the various buildings that I have worked on with Mr. Senda, this building really made sense to me in terms of lighting. We, the lighting designers, use the terms "task light" and "ambient light" or "task and ambient lights," but here in this library, I see beautiful shadows appropriately arranged in places in need, rather than illuminating the entire area. Except for the light on the work surfaces, the so-called functional light, the focus is more on the ambient light to make the best use of the scenery and the architecture. I believe that Mr. Senda has successfully achieved them in such a large space as this library architecture.

Functions are not the only requirement for a library to operate. Comfort, as Mr. Hiromura said, is crucial, and understanding what users perceive as comfortable is the key. The daylight used in this library coexists quite well with the warm colors of the "bengala" red and wood.

Senda: Regarding the daylight you just mentioned, a lack of natural light makes me very anxious. I get uncomfortable with enclosed spaces, so I prefer to keep the sky or outside environment in sight. It is desirable to have daylight as prerequisite, with the necessary light at hand.

Mende: You are not the only exception, but it seems most architects have a longing for daylight. In Louis Kahn's Light Is Theme, the Kimbell Art Museum booklet on the subject of light, his only concern was how to bring in natural light, mentioning nothing about artificial light.

Although architects tend to have an aversion to artificial spaces, and have various aspirations and visions about how to incorporate natural

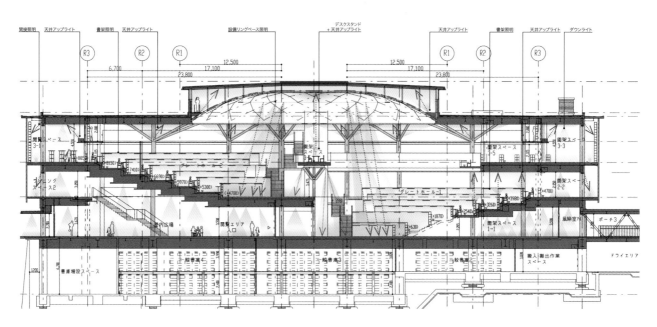

断面図に描いた照明手法スケッチ。快適な光環境を設計するには平面の照度分布図より、光の断面計画が重要になる（面出）

ただ明るいだけでなく
よい景色と共に循環していく光を
体験してほしい（面出）

好きではなくて、自然光の取り入れ方にも、いろいろな夢や希望があったりするけれど、結構間違えていることも多いんですよ。自然光を取り入れたら、これだけ明るくなるだろうと思っても、意外に明るくならなかったり、いろいろなことが起こりますから。自然光は一定ではなくて、どんどん変わっていきます。だから照度を自然光で出そうとすると、人工照明のバックアップが大切になってくる。石川県立図書館で仙田さんが取り入れたトップライトの光というのは、全体の照度を補おうということではなくて、ホールの雰囲気を生み出すための仕掛けになっているわけです。

そのほかにも一日の流れであるサーカディアンリズムを司るなど、自然光にはいろいろな役目があります。明るさだけでなく、プラスアルファがこの図書館では考えられていますね。

廣村　天井から差す光は、書架にはあまり影響がないと思うのですが、それでも時間の経過を感じることがありますね。また、書架の通路の先から少しだけ外が見えていて、外光が入ってくるのですが、夕方はものすごくきれいですよね。そういう景色としての光の演出がすてきだなと思いました。

面出　アーティフィシャルに管理されている中で自然光を感じられるというだけで、その空間は違ったものになるんですよね。

廣村　図書館には様々な年齢の方が訪れますが、具体的にどのぐらいの照度が必要かは決まっているのでしょうか。

面出　決まっていないけれど、皆がおおむね満足して、不満を持たれない照度というのは僕の経験的に、鉛直面で300ルクス出していれれば大丈夫だと思います。

ガラス張りの東京国際フォーラムでも、東京都からは300ルクス出しなさいと言われたのですが、50ルクスで、とお伝えしたんです。というのも、僕らはそれが機能的に本や雑誌が読めるようなギリギリ

light—although they often go about it in the wrong way. There can be a variety of problems, such as not being able to achieve the expected brightness with natural light. There is a need to back up the natural light with artificial lighting, if you want to produce illumination mainly by natural light, as it is not always a constant light source.

On the contrary, the natural light from the skylight that you have brought into this library is not intended to supplement the overall illumination, but rather as a means of creating ambiance in the hall.

I can also see that there are many elaborate ways to use natural light in this library, not only for brightness, but also to fulfill the various roles of natural light, such as circadian rhythm.

Hiromura: The light coming from the ceiling does not affect the bookshelves so much, but you can still feel the change of time. There is also a little glimpse of light coming in from the outdoor scenery at the end of the aisle along the bookshelves, which provides a very beautiful light in the evening. That kind of light as part of the scenery is fascinating.

Mende: Natural light can transform an artificially designed space into something different.

Hiromura: Is there a specific level of illumination required for libraries with a wide range of user ages?

Mende: Although there is no specific standard, as far as my experience is concerned, I can say that 300 lux on a vertical surface is a level of illumination that meets the needs of virtually everyone.

When we designed the Tokyo International Forum, which consists of glass walls, the Tokyo Metropolitan Government requested 300 lux, but we told them we would actually go with 50 lux. We knew this illumination level was enough to functionally read a book or magazine. And above all, the numerical value is not really of concern, as long as the ambient light is sufficient for the user to comfortably see

の照度だということを知っているし、基本的に周囲が明るく見える
ようなアンビエントライトがあれば、あまり照度が出てなくても皆
さん満足してくれるんですよ。

廣村　その辺りの頃合いが難しそうですね。やっぱり県の方は心配
するじゃないですか。

仙田　ここでも明るくしてほしいと言われましたね（笑）

面出　「面出さんはいつも暗くていいって言うけれど、もう少し明
るくしてくれないか」とよく言われますね（笑）。先ほど言ったよう
な機能的な明るさというのは最低限、読み書きしたりするために
必要なのですが。

仙田　それはサインにも関わってくる話ですよね。

廣村　"脳の意識が発火する"ようなポイントがいくつかあるんで
すよね。例えば色が派手とか、大きいとか、明るいといったことが
重要だったりするんですよ。いくら大きな文字が並んでいても、薄暗い
と見にくい、わからないと言われやすい。

今回は書架の上に文字を立てたのですが、バックボードがないので
文字に対して、どの程度の照明を当てたらいいのかが全然わからな
かったんです。サインまでの距離など、最後まで悩んで、いろいろ
テストしましたね。

面出　今、見ていても、本に当たっている照明の明るさというのは
十分だと思います。県の方からは鉛直面だけではなくて、床面照度
はどうなっていますかと尋ねられて、床面でも最低100ルクス採り
ましょうなどと照度計算をしていました。

色温度を整える
Adjusting Color Temperatures

仙田　色温度についても議論がありましたね。

面出　快適な図書館をつくるには非常に大切ですね。

仙田　内外共に、全体的にベンガラ色を基調にしようということ
は早い段階で決めていたんです。廣村さんが言ったように、白い
サインの背景としても少し濃い色味の書架にすべきではないかと
考えて、柱や梁も含め、全部濃い色味に統一しました。ただ一つ、
天井だけは、前田家成巽閣の「群青の間」にちなんで青色を使った
んです。

面出　なるほど、ベンガラ色や木の暖かい色味をきれいに見せるため
にも青も使おうということですね。僕らは仙田さんが冷たいブルー
を使うと聞いて、照明には暖かいオレンジ色を採用しました。普段
から青い光はオレンジ色の光をきれいに見せるのによく使うんですよ。
ブルーモーメントというか、空が透明な青に染まっている薄暮の

their surroundings.

Hiromura: Well, it seems to me that finding the right spot to settle the issue cannot be easily done. It surely is a concern of the prefectural administrators, isn't it?

Senda: This project was no exception (laughs).

Mende: They often say, "You always tend to make it darker, but we need a little lighter" (laughs). As I said earlier, functional luminosity means the minimum brightness required for reading and writing.

Senda: That is also related to signs, isn't it?

Hiromura: The key here is several points of neuronal firing, such as bold colors, large sizes, and brightness. Regardless of how large the letters are, people tend to complain about the dimness, saying it makes them illegible. For the signs in this project, the letters are standing on top of the bookshelves with no backboard, so we were not sure how much lighting should be applied to them at all. We have gone through various testing, such as the distance to the signs until we were satisfied with the final result.

Mende: As I look at it now, I think the lighting on the books is adequate. We calculated a minimum illuminance of 100 lux on the floor surface as well, since the prefectural administrators had asked us about the floor illuminance as well as the vertical surface.

Senda: There was also a controversy about color temperature.

Mende: Which is very important in creating a comfortable library.

Senda: From the very early stages of the project, we decided to go with a Bengala Red as the overall color scheme on both the inside and outside. The whole interior including columns and beams was uniformly finished in dark tones, figuring that the bookshelves should be colored in a slightly darker shade to serve as a background for the white sign, as Mr. Hiromura said. Only the ceiling is colored blue in reference to the Ultramarine Room in Seisonkaku, which was built by the Maeda family.

Mende: Ah, so the blue complements the warm tones of the "bengala" red and the wood. We selected the warm orange lighting to contrast with the cold blue you have chosen. I often use blue light to make orange light look beautiful. You may picture a blue moment, say, a bright orange dimly lit in a clear, blue sky. I am glad that we were able to effectively use

時間の中でポポポッと明るいオレンジ色が灯るようにするのですが、ここでもそういう組み合わせの効果を得ることができてよかったと思います。

仙田　それから廣村さんには加賀五彩を活用していただきましたね。

廣村　県の方からはベンガラ色以外でも、石川県らしさを出してほしいというお話をいただきました。一方、グレートホールのような楕円形や円形の空間では自分が今、どこにいるのかという感覚を失いがちなので、現在地をどう認識させるかと石川県らしさの表現が重要なミッションでした。

そこで、ホールをまず東西南北に分けて、その各方位を金沢の伝統色である加賀五彩で識別させたらどうかと考えました。そうしたら偶然にも天井に青色（正確には「群青の間」から着想の青ですが）が使われていたので、方位には残りの4色を配することにしたのです。

サイン計画の基本は、これらの色彩で成り立っています。色というものは対比の仕方によってきれいに見えたり、安っぽく下品に見えたりするものですが、ベンガラ色がベースにあることで、他の色が引き立てられてくると想像できました。

難しかったのは、これだけ広大な閲覧空間の中で方位がわかったとしても今、方位の中のどこにいるのかを、どのように認識してもらおうかというものです。いろいろな石川県の地名を付けてみようか、などのアイデアも出ましたが、それを覚えるのも大変だろうという話もあり、最終的に"西一の通り"のような番地表示が通りの名称になりました。来館者と管理者が共通して認識できる言葉と、サインのシステムがあることが役に立っていると思います。

this color combination here as well.

Senda: You have done a great job using Kaga-Gosai (the traditional five colors of Kaga textiles), Mr. Hiromura.

Hiromura: The request from the prefectural administrators was to create a space other than "bengala" red that is unique to Ishikawa Prefecture. They also requested us to design an effective visual expression of one's whereabouts, especially in an oval or circular space such as the Great Hall, where one can easily lose a sense of direction.

We first came up with the idea of using the traditional Kanazawa colors, Kaga-Gosai, to identify each direction from the hall, divided into four directions: east, west, south, and north. Fortunately, the ceiling happened to be blue (or more precisely, the blue inspired by the Ultramarine Room), which led us to perfectly assign the remaining four colors to each direction.

So, the signage plan is based on these five colors. Colors look very different depending on how they are contrasted, and in this case, I could visualize the "bengala" red as the base color would complement the other colors.

However, it was somehow tricky to make users recognize the detailed locations within the vast browsing space even if they knew the direction. When naming the aisle, we had several ideas, including the names of various places in Ishikawa Prefecture, but finally settled on a street address, such as "Nishiichi no Dori" (West First Street). I am sure it helps to have the signage system and language identifiable for both visitors and administrators.

広大な空間の中のどこにいるのか
「驚きつつ、動き回る」をサインで促す（廣村）

景色の連続性と居心地のよさ
Comfort Brought by the Sequentiality of the Scenery

廣村　サインを依頼される時、建築家や施主の方も何となく「わかりやすくね」とおっしゃるんですよ。それで、その人たちの望む「わかりやすい」とはどういうことかと悩む。だいたい皆さん、その先を言っていただけないんですよ(笑)

最近思うのは、わかっていないことを明らかにしていくと、わかりやすくするということがどういうことなのか、わかってくるということです。ネガティブな条件を全部出していって、それを把握できたなら、あとはそれを解決すればいい、ということになってくるわけです。

ここの図書館は大きくて、グレートホールが目立ちますが、四隅にはしっかりした書架もあるんです。そこも訪ねてもらわなければならないし、それ以外にもいろいろな施設があって、いずれも来館者にしっかりと認識していただく必要がありました。縦動線や階段もあるし、エレベーターも中2階に停まるところが何ヶ所もあって、それをわかりやすく指し示すことが最後の最後まで大変でした。

面出　建築的にはわかりづらい。でも、それをサインでどうにかして、わかりやすく示したい(笑)

廣村　よく言われるんですよ(笑)。サインでうまくわからせて、と。いや無理だろうなと思いながら、色彩の工夫をしたり、パースペクティブに見せたり。完璧ではないけれど、わかりやすさを目指したところはありました。でも、最初に言ったように、一度訪れて、回遊してもらえば、わかるし、楽しいですよね。

面出　仙田さん曰く、公園のようにめぐるということですよね。ここを訪れた人は一日中、いろいろな景色に触れて、自然光と共に一日の流れを味わうことができる。

よく僕らはシークエンシャル、連続性ということを意識します。どういう風に空間の中で、異なる視野の景色を連続させていくか。こういう景色の後に、こんな景色が来るという連続のシナリオがうまくつくれると、とても気持ちがいいんです。山を旅するのと同じような景色の連続性を建築照明デザインの原点にしているんです。

ここの図書館でも自然光を取り入れながら、様々な視野の流れというか、景色の連続が生み出されています。階段を使ったり、スロープを回っていったり、グレートホールを中心に旅するというか、めぐるのがとても楽しい空間だなと。こう回るとこっち側の外の景色が見えたり、こういう風に上がっていくとこれが見えたりと、自分が切り取っていく視野みたいなものがどうやって連続していくのか、紙芝居みたいでとても面白いなと。そして、それが快適だというのは、先ほど言ったような明るさのバランスがすごくうまく取れているということだと思います。

照明における快適というのは、単純なその場の明るさだけではなくて、跳ね返ってくる明るさと色温度が素材に合っていると気持ちが

Hiromura: Whenever an architect or owner orders signage, they ask me for "something readable," despite giving me very few details. I always have a hard time figuring out what they mean by "readable."

But I have recently come to think that the more you clarify what you don't understand, the more you realize what it means to make things easy to understand. My point is that once we have identified all the negative conditions, all you need to do is to solve them.

While the Great Hall is the focal point of this vast library, we also had to make sure that users were properly aware of the bookshelves at the four corners and the many other facilities. Therefore, I really struggled until the very end to create a clear and readable sign system for the vertical flow lines, stairways, and the several elevators that stop at the mezzanine floor as well.

Mende: This place is architecturally complex. But they want you to somehow offset that complexity with signs.

Hiromura: I get that a lot (laughs). They often ask me to reduce the complexity of space with signs. And I somehow manage to elaborate with colors and create a sense of depth, while thinking to myself that it would be impossible. I can't say for sure that sign is the optimal solution for this project, but I still tried my best to make it user-friendly. In any case, as I mentioned earlier, once you actually wander around this library, you can get a good idea of where everything is and, more importantly, it is fun.

Mende: As Mr. Senda puts it, it is like wandering around a park. This library is a great place to savor the flow of the day, surrounded by a variety of landscapes and natural light.

We frequently think of sequentiality in the design—how we provide a sequence of different views within a space. And it is intoxicating once a well-constructed scenario of sequential views has been successfully created. I take the sequential nature of similar landscapes seen while traveling in the mountains as the starting point for my architectural lighting design.

Here in the library, too, the natural light and the flow of various views—a sequence of landscapes—are well created in harmony. It is a very enjoyable space to travel around the Great Hall using the stairs and ramps. It is just like a picture-story show, with different sceneries depending on the direction you walk from, and a sequence of views you capture. On top of that, the brightness is very well-balanced and comfortable.

The key factors affecting human comfort in lighting besides illuminating the place include the compatibility of bounce-back brightness and color temperature to the material, and no glare, which is quite difficult to achieve. The great thing about this library is that these factors are consciously connected to the sequence of the landscape. Just like Mr. Hiromura's signs, it seems that the lighting also has the same effect to encourage people's urge to wander around. I thought this was a very

いいということがあります。三つ目はなかなかできないのですが、眩しさを与えないということです。この図書館では、これらの条件を意識するのと共に、だんだんと景色が変わっていくところの繋がりをうまくつくっていくことができました。廣村さんのサインも同じだと思うのですが、照明でもあっちに行ってみたくなるとか、こっち側に誘われるとか、そういうことがあるんですよね。それは今回、非常に大切なテーマだと思いましたね。

仙田　居心地という意味では、大空間だけじゃなくて、その中に小さな、柔らかい、暖かな空間がきっと必要なんですよね。そういう意味ではやはり、サインも照明も、ある種の暖かさみたいなものを発揮していると思います。

廣村　中空のブリッジの所も居心地がいいですよ。全体が見わたせるし、とどまってゆっくりするのも心地いい。あそこは照明の観点からも、そんなに明るくないですよね。明るくないからこそ、まわりの空間がよく見えるし、手元に光もあるので、本を読むには最高ですよね（笑）。この図書館における象徴的なあり方の一つだと思っているんです。

面出　これだけのものができたので、いろいろな人に見に来てほしいし、ここの光を体験してほしい。光というのは、ただ明るいだけでなくて、いい景色とともに循環していて、こんなに気持ちがいいものなのかと感じてもらえたらいいですね。

廣村　その上で図書に接する人がもっと増えてほしいし、サインのあり方にも興味を持ってもらえたらうれしいです。

面出　一つ申し上げるとすれば、照明のコントロールという意味ではまだまだ不足している部分があると思っているんです。この図書

important theme for this project.

Senda: In terms of comfort, you surely need a small, soft, warm space within the large space as much as you need a large space itself. In this case, the signs and lighting contribute to a certain kind of warmth, I think.

Hiromura: The overhead bridge, overlooking the entire area, is also a great place to relax and unwind, with the subdued lighting allowing for a clearer view of the surroundings. It's also a perfect place to read thanks to the reading light at hand (laughs). I think it is one of the values of this library's identity.

Mende: Hopefully many people will visit this beautiful architecture and experience the light. It would also be nice if they could feel that light is not only for brightness but also something comfortable as it circulates with the wonderful scenery.

Hiromura: My hope is that people will have more opportunities to get familiar with books and become interested in the value of signs through this architecture.

Mende: To add one last thing, in terms of lighting control we still have a lot of room to improve. Therefore, I would expect this library to serve as a role model in various aspects over the next five, ten, or even twenty years of its history.

Senda: In a year of operation, we should be able to identify areas for improvement in lighting through energy cost savings, operational issues, and so on. We hope to establish a system that will allow for the continuous renewal of equipment.

Mende: I look forward to working together with all of us to nurture this library through mutual guidance.

Senda: Completion of construction is not the end of the project. I would

サインも照明も「暖かさ」を発揮していて居心地のよい空間が成立している（仙田）

館が5年、10年、20年と歴史を刻んでいく中でいろいろな意味で進化していくお手本を見せていってほしいですね。

仙田　1年間運営してみて、ここの照明はこうした方がいいとか、光熱費を節約したいなど、運営上の問題も出てくるし、継続的に設備を更新していけるようなシステムをつくっていきたいですね。

面出　アドバイスをしたり、されたりして、皆でこの図書館を育てていけるようになっていくといいですよね。

仙田　でき上がっておしまいではないですからね。建物をつくっている最中の様々な苦労だとか、オープンまでに実現できなかったことなど、様々な経緯も含め、この図書館を進化させていくために、いろいろなことを伝えていく仕組みも考えていきたいと思います。

2023年1月25日収録

definitely like to think of ways to share the inside story of how the building was completed and what was not realized before the opening so that we can continue to evolve this library in the future.

Interviewed on January 25, 2023

段状のルーバー天井に覆われた屋内広場。多様な企画を行う知的
交流スペースとして活用されている。中央のメインエントランスは
文化交流エリアから閲覧エリアへの入口となる。

4階南側のリングよりグレートホールを望む。
1階まで見わたすことができ、南北に抜ける空間を確保している。

4階リングの下に1周160mの3階コンコースが備わっており、
回遊のガイドとなっている。

（上）グレートホールでは12の言葉によってカテゴリーを掲示。
（下）好奇心を刺激する段状書架。
（右）自然光を活かした空間にサインが浮かび上がる。

四角い箱と円い空間
強い軸線とWD主体
やさしい色、加賀工芸
陸と回廊.

仙台 藤森

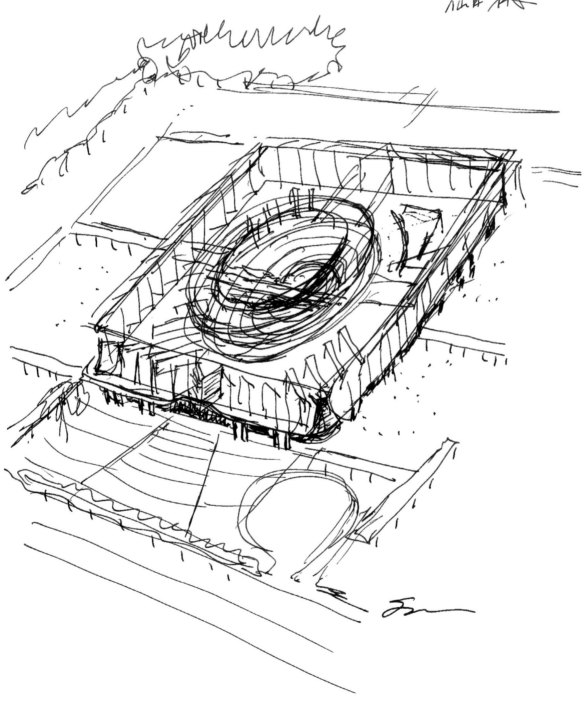

III
Good Circular Place

今、求められる「知の殿堂」とは？

What is a "Hall of Knowledge" required today?

仙田 満	✕	田村俊作	✕	植松貞夫
Mitsuru SENDA		Shunsaku TAMURA		Sadao UEMATSU
環境デザイン研究所会長		石川県立図書館館長		日本図書館協会理事長

現代の図書館が備えるべき機能や役割とは何か。

この核心的なテーマについて、石川県立図書館の基本構想検討委員会では有識者による精力的な議論がなされた。

石川県内だけでなく、日本全国の状況を踏まえ、さらには海外の動向も意識した上で浮かび上がってきた

"知の殿堂"のあり方について、三人のキーパーソンに語っていただいた。

What should a modern library offer in terms of functions and roles?

Experts vigorously debated this crucial topic for the Ishikawa Prefectural Library's foundational concept.

Considering both nationwide trends in Japan and international developments,

three key figures discussed their vision for this "Hall of Knowledge."

「石川県の」「金沢の」文化を体感する図書館

A Library to Experience the Culture of Ishikawa and Kanazawa

仙田　この図書館のコンセプトは「知の殿堂」ですが、どのような経緯でこの言葉に至ったのですか。

田村　「殿堂」というのは最初、個人的には若干面映ゆかったのですが、建物ができてみると、いかにもピッタリだと感じていますね。

仙田　プロポーザルをする側としては、少し重たいなと思っていました（笑）

植松　田村先生と私も参加した新石川県立図書館基本構想検討委員会において、当初からこの言葉が挙がっていた理由としては、いわゆるまちの図書館とは異なる、県立図書館というものをしっかりつくろう、そのためには「知」を大事にしようという委員会の総意があったものと記憶しています。

田村　昔から「県立図書館論」というものがあって、市町村立の図書館とどのように差別化するかが大きなテーマなんです。ただ、市町村で行っているようなことと別のことをやろうとしても、あまり人が集まらないのではないかという懸念がつきまとっていました。今回は図書館の基本、県立施設の使命に立ち返って、県全体に向けて読書を啓発したり、文化を振興したりするような大きな役割を担い、なおかつ、それが大勢の人を呼び込むような施設にしたいという思いがありました。

従って、単に本を読むだけの場所にはしたくなかったので、「本」ではなくて「知」を打ち出したということです。それから「殿堂」という言葉を用いたのは、皆が訪れたくなる、憧れる施設、皆にすごいねと言っていただけるような施設にしたいという思いからです。

植松　県立図書館で言えば、例えば奈良県立図書情報館は、こどもへのサービススペースは設けず、大人が対象になっています。高知県立図書館と高知市民図書館は一つの融合した建築で整備されましたが、役割分担をしっかり行おうというコンセプトで取り組まれました。そのような先例も踏まえて、ここは独立した県立図書館で全県内はもちろん、全国の利用者を集められるような図書館にしようというテーマが最初からありましたね。

仙田　そんな石川県立図書館にとって今回、県の文化が果たした役割は大きいですね。

植松　そうですね。石川県の文化を皆に理解してもらえるように、「図書館兼博物館」とか「図書館兼伝統工芸館」のような場所にしたいということも当初から言われていましたね。

田村　単に本と言っても、静かに読むようなものだけではなくて、料理本みたいに手に取って、料理をつくって初めて活きてくるような本もあるわけです。旅の本も、計画を立てて、旅先に持っていくことで活かされる。本というものは、様々な知的活動において、いろいろな使い方ができるということです。

我々も図書館の領域を知的活動全般に広げようと。そうすると石川

Senada: What led to adopting the "Hall of Knowledge" concept for this library?

Tamura: Initially, I had reservations about this term resembling "Hall of Fame", but seeing the completed building, it feels fitting.

Senada: I thought it sounded a bit heavy when we received the proposal. (laughs)

Uematsu: In the committee for the New Ishikawa Prefectural Library Plan, which Mr. Tamura and I joined, we raised this phrase early on because we aimed to define the prefectural library distinctly from city libraries, emphasizing the importance of "knowledge."

Tamura: In the past, there's been a discourse on "Prefectural Library Discussion," emphasizing its differentiation from municipal libraries. While there was a hesitation to deviate too much, fearing it might not draw people, this time we anchored ourselves to the core principles of a prefectural facility: encouraging reading and fostering culture across the prefecture.

We wanted a venue that would attract a broad audience. Hence, instead of merely being a place to read "books," we highlighted the concept of "knowledge." The choice of the term "Hall of Knowledge" was driven by our aspiration to create a facility that everyone would admire and feel compelled to visit.

Uematsu: The Nara Prefectural Library focuses on adults, lacking a children's section. The Kochi Prefectural Library and Kochi Citizens Library, while unified in architecture, maintain distinct roles. Considering these examples, the goal was a standalone library in Ishikawa to attract nationwide visitors.

Senda: Ishikawa's culture played a pivotal role for its library.

Uematsu: Indeed. From the outset, there was a desire to create a place where everyone could understand the culture of Ishikawa Prefecture, something like a "library combined with a museum" or a "library integrated with a traditional crafts center."

Tamura: When we talk about books, it's not just about silent reading. For instance, with cookbooks, they come to life when you pick them up and start cooking. Travel books become valuable when planning a trip and taking them on your journey. Books have various uses across intellectual activities.

We're looking to expand the library's purview to cover all intellectual pursuits. In Ishikawa, the bedrock of such activities lies in traditional culture; in Noto, it's the countryside and coastal landscapes. Why not anchor our efforts in these traditions? That was our initial idea.

Uematsu: There was a discussion about displaying Hideki Matsui's spikes on a bookshelf, right? (laughs). From the beginning, we approached the project with such a mindset, resulting in the showcasing of high-quality items. I believe it materialized our vision

県の知的活動のベースは伝統文化であり、能登で言えば里山・里海であり、そういった文化を活動の軸に据えてもいいんじゃないか。基本構想はそんな感じでしたね。

植松　本棚に松井秀喜氏のスパイクを収めた箱を組み込んで展示したら、という話もありましたね（笑）。最初からそういう姿勢で取り組んできて、結果的にハイレベルなものを展示することになりました。石川県の、金沢の文化を体感できるような図書館にしようという構想が具現化したものと思います。

to create a library where one can experience the culture of Ishikawa and Kanazawa.

あらゆる本やモノを活かし
ディスプレイしようと議論を重ねた（田村）

大空間で思いがけない体験を

Unexpected Experiences in a Large Space

仙田　ライブラリーとミュージアムは、ほとんど発祥が一緒ですよね。
田村　歴史的にはそうですよね。例えば大英博物館はハンス・スローンという人の個人的な趣味で集めたコレクションがもとになっていますが、それこそ博物と本とがごっちゃになっていますね。
仙田　文学者で小説家の松浦寿輝さんの『知の庭園』（筑摩書房）という本に大英博物館が出てくるんです。そこのリーディングルームがすばらしいと（笑）
植松　あの円形大閲覧室の形式はフランスの国立図書館に、そして

Senda: Libraries and museums share similar origins, don't they?
Tamura: Historically, yes. For instance, the British Museum originated from Hans Sloane's collection, a mix of artifacts and books.
Senda: The museum's reading room is mentioned in the book "*Chi No Teien (The Garden of Knowledge)*" by writer and novelist Hisaki Matsuura. That reading room is impressive (laughs).
Uematsu: That circular reading room design influenced the Bibliothèque nationale de France and Stockholm Public Library in Sweden, and even the U.S. Library of Congress has a central circular layout.

スウェーデンのストックホルム市立図書館に継承されました。アメリカ議会図書館も真ん中が円形ですね。

仙田　今回、我々も円形の図書館に取り組んだわけですが、テーマとして非常に面白いと思いましたね。当初、私は「文化交流エリア」と「閲覧エリア」という2核に分けたかたちを考えていたのですが、最終的に1核にして、文化交流エリアの下をくぐると、大空間の閲覧エリアに行けるというかたちをとりました。それが奏功したんじゃないかな。

田村　その案を見た時に正直、どうしようと思ったんですよ（笑）。そういう図書館を使いやすくすることができるのかと。日常的に本を出し入れしなければならないし、スロープで動線をつくっていくというけれど、どうなるんだろうと。

それから吹抜けの建物の場合、音がブワッと広がるので、それも大丈夫かなと。話している音が上まで広がっていくわけですが、今回はむしろ、それを逆手に取ろうと考えて「おしゃべりOK」としたのが、よかったですね。

仙田　結果的に、とてもよかったと思いますよ。

植松　でも、こんなに大きな円になるとは思わなかった（笑）

田村　最後までこのスケール感は想像できませんでしたね。本当にでき上がって初めて、文化交流エリアから閲覧エリアに入った時に「うわぁ、これはなんだ」と。それまで模型を見ていても、全然わからなかったですからね。

植松　4階の一番上からだと、だいたい1万㎡ほどのスペースが見わたせるんですよね。

仙田　そんな40×50mの空間に7万冊が入っているという。AIU（国際教養大学）の図書館は直径21mで蔵書が5万冊なんですよね。ここは直径で、その倍ぐらいあるんですよ。だからスロープの幅も3mとったのですが、全体のスケール的にもよかったと思います。

田村　仙田先生の遊環構造理論が活きていますよね。眺めていると皆さん、グルグル回っていますよ。回っていくといろいろなものに出会うという。

植松　今、なかなか思いがけない発見をするということがないんですよね。そういう体験ができるような大きな書店も少なくなってきましたし。図書館でもパソコンやスマホで予約して、取りに行くだけのような場所になっているところが多い。

本を眺めて、これがいいとか、ちょっとこっちも面白そうだ、みたいに目が移っていくような体験ができる図書館が実はあまりないんですよ。ここはスロープを使って、そういう体験ができる、すばらしい図書館だと思います。

Senda: This time we embarked on the challenge of designing a circular library, an intriguing concept. I had initially imagined splitting it into two main zones: a "cultural exchange zone" and a "reading zone." However, we ultimately combined them. Now, one moves beneath the cultural exchange zone, transitioning into a spacious reading zone. This strategy seems to have been effective.

Tamura: Seeing the initial plan, I had my reservations (laughs). I pondered its practicality, considering we'd be regularly moving books and orchestrating traffic using slopes. Moreover, open-design buildings can amplify sound. But our decision to encourage conversation inside the library, turning that potential downside around, seems to have been a good call.

Senda: Overall, I believe the endeavor was quite successful.

Uematsu: The scale of the circle did surprise me, though (laughs).

Tamura: It wasn't until completion that I could truly grasp its enormity. Entering the reading zone from the cultural exchange zone was an overwhelming experience. Even the preliminary model couldn't fully convey that feeling.

Uematsu: From the topmost level, the view encompasses about 10,000 square meters, correct?

Senda: In a space boasting a 40-meter diameter, we have 70,000 books. To compare, AIU's library, at a 21-meter diameter, houses 50,000 books. Given that our diameter is nearly double, the 3-meter width for the slope seems appropriate, aligning with the structure's scale.

Tamura: Mr. Senda, your "circular play system theory" is truly evident here. One can observe visitors navigating in circles, making novel discoveries.

Uematsu: Nowadays, stumbling upon something unexpected is becoming a rarity, especially with the decline in sizeable bookstores. Many modern libraries cater to individuals who reserve online and just collect their chosen book.

The joy of spontaneously selecting a book, thinking "This seems intriguing," is becoming less common. This establishment, with its unique sloping design, revives that lost experience. It's an exceptional library.

眠っていた本をよみがえらせる"目次"
Reviving Books: The "Table of Contents"

田村　グレートホールをどのように活かすかということを、さんざん職員の間で議論したんです。活かせるような本はもちろん、あらゆるものをディスプレイしようと。

さらに日本十進分類法では、せっかくの本が面白く見せられないから、自分たちなりに分類を考えてみようということで、12項目で行こうということになったんですね。

そこで使われている、サインにも載せたコピーですが、「石川コレクション」だけは「里の恵み・文化の香り」という風に名詞になっていますが、それ以外は全部「好奇心を抱く」みたいな動詞形なんです。中分類・小分類でも結構工夫していて、「暮らしを広げる」の中の料理本のところでは「デザートは別腹」なんて見出しを立てたりね（笑）

仙田　あれは見ているだけで楽しいですね。

田村　楽しいでしょう。一般的な図書館にも"ビジネス支援コーナー"がありますが、真面目にビジネス書が並んでいるだけなんですよね。ここでは「一刻も早く帰りたい」とかね（笑）、そういう見出しを打ち出しているんです。そこのところは司書がよく頑張っていますね。

仙田　やっぱり"目次"は重要ですよね。

田村　1階西エリアに設けた「本との出会いの窓」は目次空間みたいになっています。「世界に飛び出す」というコーナーのハワイのところに行くと、トロピカルフルーツの香りが漂ってくるんですよ（笑）。窓の後ろにわざわざ扇風機つけたりして、もう凝りに凝ってね。やっぱり職員が楽しまないと面白くならないですよ。

仙田　何でもそうですよね。学校でも、やっぱり先生が楽しんで教えないとね。

田村　ここの「こどもエリア」も、仙田先生のおかげで遊びと本が渾然一体になったような空間になりましたね。

植松　先ほどの話に戻ると、図書館でも一旦書庫に入ってしまった本は、なかなか表に出てくることがなくて、塩漬けみたいになっているのが多いんですよね。でも、ここでは書庫に入っていた本を掘り起こして、先ほどお話しいただいたようなキャッチをつけて魅力的に紹介してくれているんです。利用度が下がっていた本を生き返らせたという意味では、図書館界に与える影響は相当大きいと思います。

田村　いろいろ県立図書館を見せていただくと、どこでもだいたい、閲覧エリアよりも書庫の方が面白いんですよ（笑）。書庫に面白い本がいっぱい入っているんです。それをそのまま眠らせておくのはもったいないと、ずっと思っていたんです。

そうしたら、司書の方々が面白い本を書庫から、たくさん探し出してきたんです。それを4階の一周160mの「リング」に並べると生きるんですよね。例えば全集本を普通の閲覧エリアで見せても、全く面白くないのですが、ここでは、こんなシリーズがあったのか、と見つけて、驚いていただける。図書館関係者からも4階を訪れて

Tamura: We extensively discussed among the staff on how to make the most of the Great Hall, wanting to display not just useful books, but everything.

Given that the Japanese Decimal Classification doesn't make books as appealing, we decided on our own 12 categories.

The signs, like the one for "Ishikawa Collection," use nouns like "Blessings of the Village & Scent of Culture," but all others use verb forms, like "Spark Curiosity." We've also been creative with subcategories, for instance, under "Expanding Life," the section for cookbooks reads "Desserts Have Their Own Stomach" (laughs).

Senda: It's fun just looking at that approach.

Tamura: Isn't it? Most libraries have a "Business Support Corner" filled with serious business books. But here, we have playful headlines like "Want to Go Home ASAP" (laughs). Our librarians really put in the effort.

Senda: The "index" really matters, doesn't it?

Tamura: On the first floor's west area, there's a "Window to Encounter Books"—it's like a space with a table of contents. Go to the "Dive into the World" section, and you'll smell tropical fruits in the Hawaii area (laughs). There's even a fan placed behind the window for added effect. If the staff isn't having fun, it won't be interesting.

Senda: That applies to everything. If teachers aren't enjoying teaching, it shows.

Tamura: Thanks to you, Mr. Senda, our "Children's Area" has become a space where play and books meld seamlessly.

Uematsu: Going back to our previous topic, in most libraries, once books are stored away, they rarely see the light of day again—many become like they're "pickled" in storage. However, here, you've unearthed those stored books, adding captivating titles and showcasing them attractively. In terms of revitalizing books that had decreased in usage, I believe the impact on the library world is profound.

Tamura: When I visit various prefectural libraries, I often find that the storage areas are more intriguing than the reading zones (laughs). The storage houses many fascinating books. It's a shame to let them remain untouched.

With this realization, our librarians diligently dug out these interesting books from storage. When displayed along the 160m "Ring" on the 4th floor, they come to life. For instance, a complete series might not be appealing in a regular reading area, but here, patrons can discover and be amazed by such collections. Many library professionals who've visited the 4th floor have commented on the captivating way the books are showcased.

Senda: The aerial ring above the hall, sort of a catwalk, with books lined up—it's visually appealing.

来館者数だけでなく
生活の質や学力の向上なども
図書館の評価軸に加わってくる〔植松〕

いただくと、こんなすごい本を、こんな風に面白く並べられるんですね、という感想をいただけています。

仙田　ホール上方の空中リングというか、キャットウォーク的な仕かけになっていて、本がずらっと並んでいるというのが、絵として面白いですよね。

スケール感とデジタルの融合による可能性

Possibilities through the Integration of Scale and Digital

仙田　実際に図書館が動き出して、感じていること、問題などはありますか。

田村　やはり、ものすごく大きいということですね。図書館で資料と接するポイントはまず、興味を掻き立てられ、ブラウジングすることで、様々な出会いを楽しむということ。もう一つは特定の資料を探し出すということですが、いわゆる調べもののために図書館を使おうという人にとっては、ここの空間は大き過ぎるということがあるかもしれません。

例えば3階にレファレンスサービスのカウンターがあるのですが、そこで情報を得た人が反対側の、2階の南側などに本を取りに行こうとすると、ちょっと気が滅入るというか。そういった状況をどう

Senda: Now that the library is operational, have you noticed any issues or unique experiences?

Tamura: The vastness of the space is evident. In a library, one engages with materials by first arousing curiosity and enjoying serendipitous encounters through browsing. Another way is seeking specific materials. For those using the library for research, the space might seem too vast.

For instance, after receiving information at the 3rd-floor reference counter, one might feel a tad overwhelmed when going to fetch a book from the opposite side on the 2nd floor. That's an aspect we're considering.

Uematsu: Initially, we proposed having staff on both sides of the circumference for immediate queries. However, due to personnel

するかということがありますね。

植松　私たちも当初から、円周の両サイドに職員がいて、利用者が
すぐ質問できるようにするべきだということを言っていたのですが、
そこまでの数の職員は配置できないということで、東側に集中させ
ようということになったんですね。これについては県の方々も、円の
大きさをあまり理解できていなかったと思うんです。

仙田　利用者がここまで増えるということも、予測できなかったかも
しれませんね。

田村　これだけ圧倒的な量の本が、面を見せて並んでいる迫力は全く
想像がつかなかったです。この迫力、スケール感とデジタルをどの
ように融合させていくかということも、これからの図書館を考えた
時に大事になってきますね。

植松　Wi-Fiはしっかり整備されているんですよね。

田村　Wi-Fiはもう自由に使えるようになっていますね。「知の殿
堂」とデジタルとの関係でいうと、 SNSでの評価、コメントはもち
ろん、音楽ユーチューバーに演奏してもらったり、様々なことを試し
ています。これまで行われてきたような電子書籍の提供に留まらない、
多様な可能性が開かれているということがだんだんわかってきました。

limitations, we decided to concentrate them on the east side. I
believe the prefecture officials didn't quite grasp the enormity of
the circle.

Senda: Perhaps they didn't anticipate the surge in users.

Tamura: The awe one feels seeing this sheer volume of books displayed
face-out was beyond our imagination. Integrating this grand scale with
digital is pivotal for the future of libraries.

Uematsu: The Wi-Fi is fully functional, right?

Tamura: Yes, Wi-Fi is freely available. Speaking of the relationship
between this "Hall of Knowledge" and digital, we are exploring various
possibilities: ratings and comments on social media, collaboration with
music YouTubers, and more. We're realizing it goes beyond traditional
e-book offerings.

居場所としての図書館の"楽しさ"

The "Fun" of Libraries as a Place to Be

仙田　図書館という空間では、皆が同じ時間を過ごしているんですよね。それぞれ行っていることはパーソナルなことなのだけれど、同じ時間を同じ場所で過ごしているというのが楽しみでもあるんです。この間、タクシーに乗ったら、運転手さんの息子が毎日のように、ここの図書館に通っていると言うんですよ。息子の勉強も以前の2、3倍ははかどってる、なんて言ってた（笑）

田村　石川県の学力が上がってくれたらね、もうこちらとしても言うことはない（笑）

植松　これまで図書館を評価する際の基準としては、来館者数や貸出冊数というものがお決まりだったのですが、これからは生活の質を向上させるとか、学力が上がるとか（笑）、あるいは周辺の土地が値上がりするとか、そういったことも含めて評価していくことが必要になってくると思いますね。

仙田　図書館がまちづくりや地域活性化などの非常に重要なツールになりつつあるのではないですか。

植松　図書館はあらゆる年齢層の人を対象にしていますからね。その上、入場無料で予約もいらない、好きなだけいられるという場所は他にはないんですよね。どんな図書館でもしっかり運営すれば、一定の人通りが得られるという、いわば集客力の高い施設なんですよ。

仙田　やっぱり居場所というかな。ずっと居続けても、誰からも文句を言われない。居続けられる場所というのがすごく重要だと。

植松　今日はちょっと体調が悪いから図書館にいようとか。今日は前向きな気持ちだから図書館にいたいとか。だから今日はこの辺に座ろうとか、いろいろな気分で居場所を選べますしね。

仙田　安心基地であり、挑戦のためのステップでもあるというか、それが合わさったものが図書館ですよね。

植松　同じ趣味の人の会や、世代を超えたグループができたりするといいですよね。

田村　本を核にしていても、実は様々な過ごし方ができるということですね。

仙田　私は学校でも図書館が重要だと言っているんです。学校の中で安心できる唯一の居場所が図書室とか図書館なんだ。これから、ますます大事になってくると思うんです。

植松　残念ながら、学校の図書室に職員が常に在籍しているケースは多くないんです。鍵がかかっていることが普通というところも少なくないんですね。

仙田　学校図書館をもっと開放しろと言っているのですが（笑）

田村　むしろ、学校の真ん中に図書館を配置して、そこに人が出入りして、活動したり、くつろいだりというのが望ましい。

植松　オープンスクール型の学校は、そうした方がいいですよね。

仙田　軽井沢の風越学園というのが2020年に開校したのですが、

Senda: In the space of a library, everyone spends the same time, don't they? While what they're doing is personal, there's a sense of enjoyment in sharing the same place at the same time.

I recently took a taxi and the driver told me that his son visits this library almost every day. He mentioned that his son's studies have progressed two to three times faster than before. (laughs)

Tamura: If this improves academic performance in Ishikawa Prefecture, we couldn't ask for more. (laughs)

Uematsu: Traditionally, metrics for evaluating libraries have been the number of visitors and the number of books lent. But in the future, we need to consider improvements in quality of life, increases in academic performance (laughs), or even an increase in local land values.

Senda: Isn't the library becoming an essential tool for town-building and regional revitalization?

Uematsu: Libraries target people of all ages. Moreover, it's a place that doesn't require a fee, or booking, and you can stay as long as you like. So, if managed well, any library can attract a lot of visitors.

Senda: It's about providing a place where people can stay continuously without any complaints. It's crucial to have such places.

Uematsu: Depending on how they feel on a particular day, people can choose to be in the library. Whether they're feeling a bit under the weather or in a positive mood, they can decide where to sit and spend their time.

Senda: Libraries are both a safe base and a step for challenges.

Uematsu: It would be nice if groups are formed based on shared interests or across generations.

Tamura: Even centered around books, there are various ways to spend time.

Senda: I always say that libraries are essential in schools. The only place where students feel at ease in school is the library or the reading room. I believe its importance will only grow.

Uematsu: Unfortunately, it's not common for school libraries to have permanent staff. Many are locked and not accessible.

Senda: I keep saying they should open up school libraries more! (laughs)

Tamura: Ideally, a library should be at the center of a school, with people coming and going, engaging in activities or relaxing.

Uematsu: Open-school models would indeed benefit from this approach.

Senda: There's a school called Karuizawa Kazakoshi Gakuen that opened in 2020, where the library is the central focus. It feels as if there are classrooms within the library.

Tamura: Speaking of nearby locations, there's an establishment in Nonoichi City called "Manabi no Mori Nonoichi Kaleido." There,

そこはとにかく図書館が中心。図書館の中に教室があるぐらいの感じなんですよ。

田村　ここの近所で言うと、野々市市の「学びの杜ののいちカレード」という施設がやはり、図書館がコアにあって、美術館的なスペースもあれば、公民館的な部屋もあるというつくりになっていますね。

the library is at the core, with spaces that feel like art museums and rooms resembling community centers.

日本のスタンダードを超える、新しい県立図書館像
A New Vision for Prefectural Libraries That Goes Beyond Japan's Standards

仙田　日本の図書館の歴史において、石川県立図書館はどのように評価されるでしょうか。

植松　私は国内で、相当たくさんの図書館を見てきましたが、新しい図書館建築と新たなサービスのかたちを提案したという意味で、大きな意義があると思いますね。

田村　図書館という施設がどんなものであるべきなのかという意味で、いろいろなものがここで提案されている気がするんですよね。

まず、先ほどから述べているように、ここは単なる読書施設ではないということ。次にこれまでも見栄えはいいけれども、使い勝手はどうなのかという図書館がありましたが、ここは見栄えだけでなく、様々な使い方ができるし、その意味で、これまでの県立図書館のあり方とは相当異なるものを提案できていると思います。

植松　県内からここにいらっしゃった方から、我がまちにも、もうちょっと、しっかりした図書館が欲しいとか、こういう図書館にすべき、といった声が上がってくることが望まれますね。そうすると県内全体の図書館の底上げにもなりますし。

田村　SNSを見ていると、本なんか読んだことないけれど、面白そうだから来た、みたいな方が結構いらっしゃるんですよ。何年ぶりかに本を手に取ったとか、そんな声もありますね。

植松　全然、図書館を知らなかったような人たちですよね。

田村　それでいいんだと思うんですよ。そういう風にして、知的なものに接することの楽しさみたいなものを、ここで感じでほしい。それが各市町村の図書館の利用にも繋がってくれれば、県立図書館としての役割を果たしたことになるのではないかと思います。

――国際的な位置づけという意味では、いかがでしょうか。

田村　ここは何より美しい建築ですし、運営面でも、いい線を行っているのではないかという気がします。その意味では、日本国内のスタンダードな図書館のあり方を超えているのだと思いますね。例えば、北欧諸国の図書館ではバリアフリーがかなり徹底しているの

Senda: In the history of Japanese libraries, how is the Ishikawa Prefectural Library evaluated?

Uematsu: Having visited numerous libraries in Japan, I think the Ishikawa Prefectural Library holds great significance. It brings forth a new library architecture and a novel service model.

Tamura: I think it proposes several new ideas in terms of how a library should be as a public facility.

It's not just a reading facility. Some libraries looked good but weren't necessarily functional. This one, however, is both aesthetically pleasing and versatile. It offers something quite different from traditional prefectural libraries.

Uematsu: I hope visitors from within the prefecture will express a desire for such comprehensive libraries in their own towns, which would elevate the standards of all libraries in the prefecture.

Tamura: When I look at social media, I see many people who say they haven't read a book in a while but came here because it seemed interesting. There are comments from people saying it's been years since they last picked up a book.

Uematsu: These seem to be people who aren't familiar with libraries at all.

Tamura: And that's perfectly fine. I hope that they can experience the joy of engaging with intellectual content here. If that encourages them to use the libraries in their own towns, then the Ishikawa Prefectural Library has fulfilled its role.

——In terms of its international standing, how would you evaluate it?

Tamura: Architecturally, it's a beauty. In terms of operation too, I believe we're doing quite well. It certainly goes beyond the standard Japanese library. For instance, Nordic libraries excel in barrier-free accessibility, and I feel we've achieved that here to a considerable extent.

It aligns with European or international trends, promoting a broader "world of knowledge."

ですが、ここでもかなりのレベルで実現できていると思います。

また、当初からテーマに掲げている「知」の世界が広がっている図書館という意味でも、ヨーロッパ寄りと言いますか、国際的な動向に沿っているのではないかと思います。

植松　"知の広場"になっていますよね。アントネッラ・アンニョリの『知の広場』という本がありますが、彼女が言っているのは、誰もが集まってこられるような広場であり、知識が得られる場所という感じですね。

田村　本が必ずしもメジャーなコミュニケーションツールではなくなった時代に、図書館に意味があるとしたら何なのか。そういうことを考えた時に、このような一種の"知の広場"みたいなものが大事になってきたのだと思いますね。

デジタルの時代だからこそ、集まってくることに意味があるし、"気づき"がすごく大事なんですよね。ここに来たら気づけるという。デジタル一辺倒だと、なかなか難しいですからね。

仙田　そうですね。やっぱり人が成長していく過程の中で、小さい頃から図書館でいろいろ体験したことは、後々大きな意味を持つと思いますよ。

植松　そう。図書館に通った経験を携えて、成長していったらいいですよね。いい思い出になると思いますし。

田村　こどもエリアで、遊びながら本を読む体験をして。そこからスムーズに、だんだんと広いドームの方に移っていってほしい。

植松　絶対に、しっかり本を読む人になるんじゃないですか（笑）

仙田　本が好きな人にね。やっぱり本を好きになってもらわないといけません。

2023年4月21日収録

Uematsu: Yes, it's like a "plaza of knowledge." Agnoli Antonella speaks of a plaza in her book "Le piazze del sapere," where everyone gathers and knowledge is shared.

Tamura: In an era where books are no longer the primary communication tool, what then is the significance of a library? I believe that it has evolved into something akin to a "plaza of knowledge."

Precisely because it's the digital age, gathering holds value. "Realizations" are paramount. Coming here offers insights that are elusive in a purely digital environment.

Senda: Experiences in a library, especially from childhood, hold profound meaning in one's growth.

Uematsu: Absolutely. Growing up with memories of frequenting a library is enriching. It becomes a cherished memory.

Tamura: I wish children, through play and reading in the dedicated kids' area, gradually transition to the broader dome section of the library.

Uematsu: If they start here, they'll definitely grow into avid readers, right? (laughs)

Senda: It's essential for them to develop a love for books. That should be the goal.

Interviewed on April 21, 2023

様々なイベントが開催されるだんだん広場。読書や学習など、来館者にとって魅力的な居場所ともなっている。

グレートホール1階。本の目次とグラビアのように
「本との出会いの窓」をディスプレイしている。

（上）「本との出会いの窓」のコーナーを1/15勾配のスロープで登っていく。
（下）4階の空中リング。これまで書庫で眠っていたような貴重な本に出会える。

専門開架書架はグレートホールの三つの隅に展開される。書架の
間の通路はグレートホールの反対側の外壁に向き合っている。

（左）グレートホール中央部。上はブリッジ、下はソファベンチ。ガラスには段状書架が映り込む。

（上）文化交流エリア2階のラウンジ。

（下）4階リングにも居場所を設置。3階の閲覧室が覗ける。

親子連れが利用しやすいように、書棚と遊具が一体となったこどもエリア。

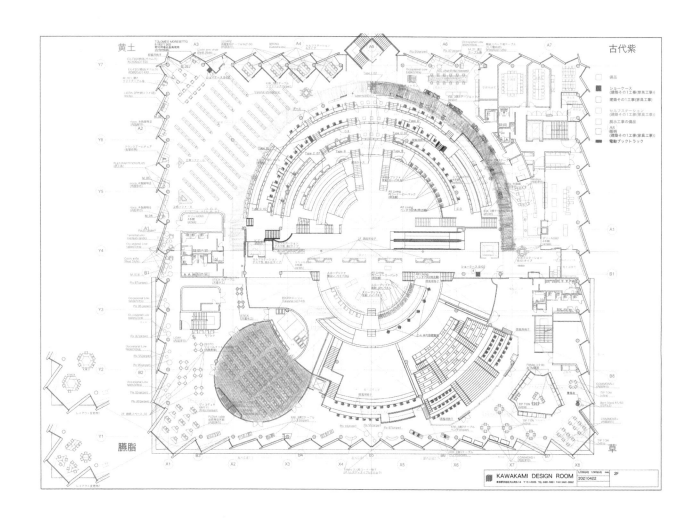

ところで一番好きな席は？
野暮な問いだね！
ベタな答えだけど、
出来の良い子もよくない子も皆可愛いように
椅子もそれぞれ多様な居場所を
得ていると信じたいね！

川上元美

IV
Square and Hole

他者と出会い、未知の文化に触れるための居場所とは？

What is a place to encounter new people and experience unknown cultures?

嘉門佳顯
Yoshitaka KAMON

石川県県民文化スポーツ部
文化振興課専門員
※取材時

×

仙田 満
Mitsuru SENDA

環境デザイン研究所会長

×

川上元美
Motomi KAWAKAMI

川上デザインルーム代表

書架やデスク、ソファ、椅子など、石川県立図書館では、そのインテリアにも、
建設に携わった多くの人々の思いやこだわりが込められている。
本と家具、さらには来館者のライフスタイルをいかに結びつけていくのか？
色使いから肌触りまで、多角的な観点から語っていただいた。

In the bookshelves, desks, sofas, chairs, and interior, the passion and attention to detail of the many involved in constructing the Ishikawa Prefectural Library are imbued.
How does one tie books, furniture, and the lifestyles of visitors together?
We hear various perspectives from the architects, from color use to texture.

"窓辺"の可能性と加賀五彩

Kaga-Gosai and the Potential of the "Window-side"

仙田　プロポーザルが通った時、植松（貞夫）さんに会いに行ったんですよ。そうしたら「仙田さん、家具のデザインはどうするの?」と言われたのですね（笑）

国際教養大学の図書館の時は、家具までE.D.I.（環境デザイン研究所）でデザインしたんです。でも、今回は、20代の頃から親しくしていた川上さんにお願いしました。石川県立図書館では本と家具と空間との関係性、グレートホールとの距離感というものが、とてもうまく設定できたんじゃないかと思います。

ここでは、表紙が見えるように本を"面陳"しているのが、本の見え方、見せ方という意味では象徴的です。

川上　あれだけ本の見え方が違うのかということで、私も感激しました。

実は仙田さんも結構、椅子をつくっておられるんですよね。

仙田　「思考椅（しこうき）」とかね。考える椅子。

川上　それに家具や遊具も繋がってきて、独特の世界観を仙田さんは持っている（笑）

仙田さんから、大仕事をしようよと声をかけていただき、不思議な縁を感じます。石川県とは「フードピア金沢」という催しが1985年から始まりましたが、それに関わったのが最初です。また、加賀市のもとで磯崎（新）さん設計の「中谷宇吉郎 雪の科学館」が主催した「雪のデザイン賞」や、「国際漆展・石川」などの公募展の審査に関わったり、金沢美術工芸大学の客員教授を10年ほど務めたりもしておりました。

そんな経緯もあって今回、この図書館に関わることになったのですが、変なことはできないなと（笑）。もう、心して臨みましたね。

仙田　東京でアドバイザーの先生方や、私と川上さんとで一緒に意見交換会に出たことがありましたね。

嘉門　プロポーザルの審査員を務めた先生方に、設計が始まってからも石川県立図書館の整備に関するアドバイザーとして県が委嘱し、香山（壽夫）先生と植松（貞夫）先生、竺（覚暁）先生、現在館長を務めている田村（俊作）という4名の方々に、県がアドバイスを伺いにいくという体制をつくっていました。その中で、仙田先生や川上先生からアドバイザーの方々に直接説明していただくという機会があったわけです。

仙田　竺覚暁先生がお元気で、本当にお世話になりました。香山先生には「自分は"端の空間"がきっと、すごく好きになるだろう」とおっしゃっていただきました（笑）

嘉門　実施設計の初期の段階で、東京・平河町の都道府県会館にお集まりいただいて。平面図なり断面図なりを見ていただいた時に、窓辺という空間のポテンシャルを香山先生が指摘されたんですよね。そこから窓辺に力を入れよう、というギアが入ったものと記憶

Senda: When the proposal was approved, I visited Mr. Uematsu (Sadao). I was subsequently asked, "Mr. Senda, what will you do for the furniture design?" (laughs).

E.D.I.(Environment Design Institute) designed even the furniture for the Akita International University (AIU) library. But this time, I asked Mr. Kawakami, a close friend since my twenties. For Ishikawa Prefectural Library, I think we very successfully created the relationship between the books, furniture, and space, and distance from the Great Hall.

Here, the books are "displayed face-out," symbolic of the way books are seen and shown.

Kawakami: I was also amazed by just how differently the books appeared.

Mr. Senda, you actually make chairs quite a bit too, right?

Senda: Yes, like the "Thought Chair." A chair for thinking.

Kawakami: Add playground equipment to the furniture, and you get Mr. Senda's unique worldview (laughs).

When I think of the big job request from Mr. Senda, I sense a strange destiny. I got involved with Ishikawa Prefecture for the first Foodpia Kanazawa event in 1985. I judged public exhibitions like The Ishikawa International Urushi Exhibition, and Snow Design Competition by the Nakaya Ukichiro Museum of Snow and Ice, designed by Arata Isozaki, for Kaga City. I was also a guest lecturer at Kanazawa College of Art for about ten years.

And so, through this sequence of events, I got involved with this library. I knew I couldn't do anything strange, though (laughs). I approached it with care.

Senda: You once attended discussions in Tokyo with the advisors, myself, and Mr. Kawakami, didn't you?

Kamon: After starting the design, the prefecture entrusted the professors who were judges for the proposals to be advisors for the development of the Ishikawa Prefectural Library. The prefecture received advice from Mr. Hisao Kohyama, Mr. Sadao Uematsu, Mr. Kakugyo Chiku, and Mr. Shunsaku Tamura, the current director. Dr. Senda and Dr. Kawakami could talk directly to the advisors in that meeting.

Senda: Dr. Kakugyo Chiku is doing well and was of great help to us. Mr. Kohyama assured me he would come to like the "border space" very much (laughs).

Kamon: Early in the detailed design phase, we gathered at the Prefectural Hall in Hirakawacho, Tokyo. When we examined the floor plan and section drawings, Dr. Kohyama noted the potential of the window-side spaces. I remember that from then, we really focused on the window-sides.

Senda: After that, the Building Management Division had the idea to utilize the "Kaga-Gosai," meaning five colors of Kaga, when possible for the interior.

しています。

仙田　それから、営繕課のアイデアで館内に「加賀五彩」をできるだけ使おうと。

川上　いいアイデアになりましたね。その後、仙田さんの提案でさらに、天井に成巽閣の「群青の間」にちなんだ青色を用いることにもなりました。内外観のベンガラ色も含め、これらがうまく機能して、石川らしさを表すことができました。

仙田　ああいう色を、公共建築で使う機会はなかなかないと思います。

川上　加賀五彩の"藍色"については、館内の一部に本物の藍色が使えないかと県の方からオファーがありましたね。天然ウルトラマリンブルーであるラピスラズリの石を削って粉にしたものを用いるのですが、それはさすがに高価で使えなかった（笑）。そういったカラーリングについて、加賀五彩は一つの方向性を示してくれました。

嘉門　それについては営繕課が施工の現場における調整も含めて、本当に頑張ったからこそ実現できたというところですね。加賀五彩によってルールが統一されたことで、道がはっきり開けた感じです。

Kawakami: It turned out to be a great idea. Mr. Senda also suggested blue for the ceiling, referencing the Ultramarine Room of Seisonkaku. These, coupled with the "bengala" (red oxide) color of the interior and exterior, functioned well together to express Ishikawa's character.

Senda: You don't often get many chances to use those types of colors in public buildings.

Kawakami: As for the Kaga-Gosai's indigo blue color, the prefectural government asked us if we could use real indigo in parts of the library. It is made from powder grounded from the natural ultramarine blue lapis lazuli stone, but in the end, because it was just too expensive, we didn't use it (laughs). Regarding that type of coloring, the Kaga-Gosai helped us with a direction.

Kamon: It was possible because the Management Division worked incredibly hard, including coordinating work at the construction site. Under the rules unified by the Kaga-Gosai, the way felt clear.

建築と家具を総合的に考える
Considering Architecture and Furniture Comprehensively

仙田　書架については、原寸模型をつくりましたね。

川上　推奨される県産材を探すとやはり、ヒバやスギなんですよね。そうした地元の材料も用いて原寸模型をつくってみて、木の色調について検討を重ねましたが、やはり暗めの方がいいなということになりましたね。

仙田　独自の分類のテーマを表すサインは白くして、書架の上に"見出し"として設置したのですが、全体としてはできるだけ落ち着いた色味にしたいと思っていました。最終的に素材を活かしつつ、いい塩梅になったのではないかと思います。

国際教養大学の書架と、今回の書架の一番大きな違いは手すりなんです。手すりの下にライトを入れたので、書架の下段の本も明るく照らしています。あれは結構、成功したんじゃないかな。

川上　グレートホールの書架では表紙を見せているわけですが、そこに光が当たると立体的に浮き出て見えるんです。何か訴えかけてくるような印象がありますね。

仙田　司書の方々による選りすぐりの本が、グレートホールの上段にある書架で表紙を見せてくれているわけです。それが段状になって、7万冊のボリューム感が出てきたのが、すごくよかったなと思います。それから興味を持った本を手に取って、そばの椅子に座って読むことができる。そこで30分、40分でも過ごせるという距離感、関係

Senda: You made a full-scale mock-up for the bookcases, didn't you?

Kawakami: When you look for the prefecture's recommended lumber, it remains cypress and Japanese cedar. Using these local materials, we made a full-size model, and after much consideration regarding the wood's tone, we agreed that a darker color was better.

Senda: The signs placed as "headlines" above the bookshelves, indicating the category themes were made white, but as a whole, we sought to keep the colors as muted as possible. I think we found a good balance as we continued to take full advantage of the materials.

The most significant difference between the AIU's bookcases and these is the hand-railing. We installed lighting under the railing so the books on the lower shelves are also well-lit. I think it was very successful.

Kawakami: The books in the Great Halls's bookcases have their front covers displayed, so when light hits them, they appear like floating objects. It gives the impression that it is appealing to you somehow.

Senda: The librarians' choice of books are displayed face-out on the bookshelves at the upper levels of the Great Hall. I think it is great that you can feel the volume of the 70,000 books because of the stepped levels.

From there, you can pick a book that attracts you, sit in the chair by your side, and read. The feeling of distance and connection for being able to spend 30, even 40 minutes there was created quite successfully. In that

どんな人がどのように滞在するのか
様々な空間と椅子のあり方を検討しました（川上）

性がうまく設定できたのではないか。そういう意味で、館内のいろいろな場所に、様々な椅子が置かれているというのはすばらしいですね。

川上　目的を持って特定の本を取りに行くのではなくて、たまたま、そこにあったものに興味を持って、「これは面白そうだ」と立ち止まり、坐して読みふけることで新しい発見がある。

仙田　国際教養大学の図書館は大学の施設ですから、閲覧席にテーブルが付いているんです。今回はソファも設置するなど、リラックスするという要素を重視していて、座るだけのバラエティに富んだ椅子もたくさん置かれています。

川上　特にグレートホールの書架について補足すれば、本の分類を通常の日本十進分類法（NDC）ではなくて、独自の12のテーマによって分類し、面陳されていることが大きいですね。分類がコンテンポラリーな言葉で理解できるし、キャッチーな言葉が心に刺さり、ハッとして立ち止まる。そこで新しい出会いや気づきが生まれるわけです。

こういったソフトというか、サービス面のアイデアはどういうところから来たのか。当然、内容が問われるし、ある程度の期間の中でも変化させていくわけでしょう。その準備を考えると、司書の方々の作業は本当に大変だろうと思いますし、プレッシャーがあるだろうけれども、図書館にとっては大変よいことですよね。これからの図書館は本の閲覧、貸出だけでなく、次のアクションまで考慮することが求められます。まさに県民に開かれた「知の殿堂」として期待されるところですね。

嘉門　計画の当初から、これだけ大きなプロジェクトなので「"多くの人が来る"ということを必ず実現するように」という指示が、知事からありました。人が来るということ、普段図書館を利用していない層

respect, it is wonderful that different chairs are placed in various places in the library.

Kawakami: Rather than purposefully going to take a specific book, you get intrigued by what you find there, by chance. You stop and think, "This looks interesting," sit down, read it, and make new discoveries.

Senda: The Akita International University library is a university building, so tables were provided for the reading seats. This time, importance was placed on relaxation, with sofas and a variety of sit-only chairs installed.

Kawakami: Additionally, regarding the Great Hall's bookshelves, the books are not classified according to the generally used Nippon Decimal Classification (NDC) but according to twelve unique themes displayed on the shelves. This is quite impactful. Classifications can be understood in contemporary terms; the catchy phrases make you stop with interest and stick with you. New encounters and discoveries are made.

Where did this "software," or rather, service idea come from? Naturally, the contents will be asked about, and changes will have to be made after a certain amount of time. The work of the librarians is likely quite difficult with a lot of pressure, considering the required preparation, but I think it is excellent for the library. Future libraries will be expected to not only provide books to read and borrow, but also take into account visitors' next actions. It is anticipated to be a true "Hall of Knowledge," opened to the prefecture's citizens.

Kamon: From the beginning of the plan, because it is such a big project, the governor directed the staff to "ensure that no doubt, many people will come." It made me think deeply about what it means to have people go to a library, and what is needed to draw even those who do not usually use it.

When Mr. Senda agreed to lead the design, we had an anticipation that a fun space would be created, and I wanted to cherish the expectation.

も引きつけることとはどういうことなのか、それを徹底的に考えました。仙田先生に設計をお願いすることになり、楽しい空間がつくられるのかな、という期待感が生まれ、それを大事にしたいと思いました。回遊的な大きな空間構成がもたらす、動き回る楽しさだったり、ワクワク感だったり、動的な魅力を持った図書館になることが基本設計の中で見えてきました。

加えて、図書館における居住性、ずっと滞在したくなるような居心地のよさや、何度も訪れたくなるような魅力が備わっているべきだということも、植松先生をはじめとする基本構想の検討委員の方々から、ずっと伺ってきました。

例えば「ヨーロッパでは、ふらっと訪れて、心地よく過ごして帰って、また明日も来るという、日常の一部として図書館があるんだ」ということを言われると、家具のように身体に近く、肌に触れるものと本を読む行為との関係の豊かさを、日本ではまだ十分に追求できていないのではないか、と考えるようにもなりました。

いわゆる建物自体については、営繕課という建築の技術職員が向き合います。でも、家具は一般的に備品として扱われますから、その範疇に含まれない。事務方としては、そんな発注上の区分によらず、建築と家具がきちんと相乗効果を発揮するよう、総合的にとらえる必要があると感じました。

仙田　今回は、発注者側に嘉門さんがおられたことがすごく大きいね。

嘉門　川上先生に家具まわりを丁寧にフォローしていただけるということになったので、県としては、その可能性を潰すようなことはしてはならない、このチャンスを活かしたいということをずっと意識していました。

川上　打合せの過程で夢を語り合ったことがありましたね。こんな

In the preliminary design, it became clear that the library would become a dynamic, fascinating place because of its big, circular configuration, where people could move about with enjoyment.

What's more, Mr. Uematsu and other members of the panel who examined the preliminary concept kept mentioning that the space should be livable, comfortable, and so inviting that people would want to stay and revisit time and time again.

For example, I was told, "In Europe, there are libraries where people casually visit, comfortably spend time, go home, and come back the following day—a part of daily life." I started to feel that Japan had not yet fully pursued the rich relationships between the act of reading and things like furniture that are close to one's body and touch the skin.

The actual building itself is dealt with by the technical staff of the Management Division. But furniture is usually regarded as fixtures and not included in their job scope. From our side, I felt we needed a more holistic approach, regardless of the order classification, in order for the architecture and furniture to blend together well.

Senda: Having Mr. Kamon on the client's side this time was very big.

Kamon: Because it was arranged that Mr. Kawakami would closely follow up with us regarding the furniture, the prefecture was always conscious not to do anything that would shut down this route, and to make the best of this opportunity.

Kawakami: We talked about our dreams during the course of our meetings. Saying, wouldn't it be great to have things like this? In any case, even from the administration side, there was broad but meticulous research and examination of what libraries should offer and a very clear view of what was needed. Then again, the prefecture's residents are highly aware of the arts and culture. There is a facility called Kanazawa

家具のように肌に触れるものと
本の関係を追求したかった（嘉門）

ものがあったらいいんじゃないかって。とにかく行政側でも、これからの図書館のあり方に関して、広い視野で周到な調査・研究をされていて、何が必要か、実に明快な視座がありました。一方で、県民の芸術や文化に対する意識が高い。金沢市民芸術村という施設がありますが、市民が自立運営しているんですよね。芸術や工芸の発表の場というより、むしろ伝習の場というのかな。できてから既に二十数年続いているのですが、そういう活動は類を見ません。

今回も、そういった県民の意識に助けられた気がしますね。石川の文化的な土壌を前提にして今、何が求められているのかということを、正攻法で考え、取り組みました。

Citizens' Art Center, self-managed by the citizens. Instead of a place that presents arts and crafts, it can be called a place of learning. Since opening, it has continued for over 20 years, but these activities remain unparalleled.

This time, too, I feel we were saved by this kind of awareness from the residents. Based on Ishikawa's culture, we used a straightforward approach to consider what is required at this moment.

様々な過ごし方に対応する椅子のバリエーション
Various Chairs Supporting Various Ways to Spend Time

仙田 やっぱり長く居続けられる場所というのは、大人やこどもを問わず、身体にフィットして柔らかくて包み込むような環境、空間なんです。でも、それは、なかなか建築自体では実現できないんですよ。

「座る」「触れる」といった場面で発揮される家具の力は、"安心の基地" の要素として非常に強いのです。本を読む時も、仕事をする時も、ゆったりとさせてくれるというのは、やっぱり家具の力だと思うのですね。

川上 「読む」という行為への入り込み方にはいろいろなタイプがあって、人によっても、その日の気分によっても異なります。図書館においても、学習するために机に向かっている人がいれば、リラックスしたい人もいるし、昼寝をしに来る人がいるかもしれないし（笑）、様々な過ごし方を想定しました。と言いながら、使う素材は少し硬めにしなければなりません。公共図書館ではものすごい使用頻度になりますからね（笑）。すなわち、家具に付きまとってくる「道具性」があるんです。いつまでも当初の状態が保てるものではないので、長いスパンを見据え、そういったことも考慮しながらデザインを検討しました。

例えば椅子に用いるファブリックを加賀五彩の色に沿って選定するのですが、生地にはピンからキリまであるわけです。当然、特注仕様になり、予算との兼ね合いを含め、どのように実際の使用状況とのバランスを取るのか、ということが結構ありました。

仙田 窓辺にファブリックの風合いを生かした衝立があるでしょう。正直言って建築家は、なかなかああいう風にはできません。空間を柔らかくする装置として、すごく魅力的ですよね。

川上 確かに安堵感というか、窓辺の各コーナーが外に開かれつつ、

Senda: As I thought, regardless of being an adult or child, a place where one can stay for a long time is an environment and space that softly embraces and fits your body. But using architecture itself makes this difficult to achieve.

The power of furniture, shown by the act of sitting and touching, is in the extraordinarily strong feeling of a "safe base" that it creates. Indeed, furniture has the power to make us comfortable when we read a book, or do work.

Kawakami: There are multiple ways to get into the act of reading, depending on the person and their mood that day. We imagined the various ways one can spend time even in a library: some visitors might sit at desks to study, some would just like to relax, and some might even come to take a nap (laughs). That said, the materials we used must have had a bit of hardness. Because it is used so frequently in public libraries (laughs). In other words, there is a sense of "equipment" associated with furniture. Since their initial condition cannot be kept indefinitely, we considered the design in terms of longevity while keeping these challenges in mind.

For example, we matched fabric colors for chairs according to the colors of Kaga-Gosai, but there are endless amounts of textures. Naturally, the specifications became custom, so we had to consider how to balance the budgetary constraints with actual usage quite a bit.

Senda: There are partitioning screens using fabric texture near the window-sides, right? To be honest, architects struggle to create something like that. It is such an ideal device to soften the space, isn't it?

Kawakami: Indeed, a sense of reassurance; each window-side "corner" opens up to the outside while being lightly compartmentalized inside, and the book- and craft shelves give a welcoming, relaxed atmosphere.

Senda: As you stated earlier, it is so important that, from the user's side,

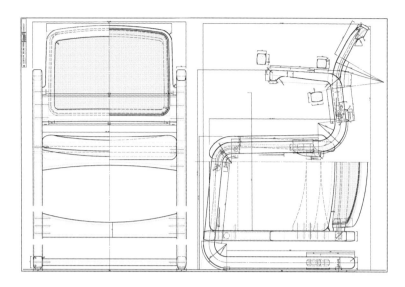

閲覧用椅子原寸図

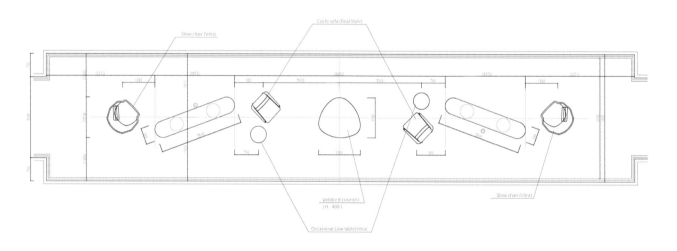

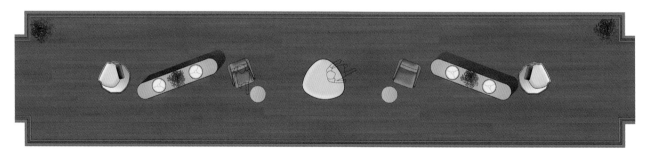

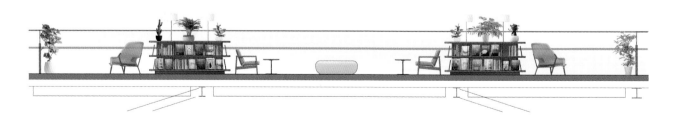

3階閲覧エリアのブリッジに設置された家具のイメージ

内に軽く仕切られ、書架や工芸棚が居心地のよい、ホッとした空気感を生み出しましたね。

仙田　先ほどおっしゃったように、利用する側としては、気持ちの持ち方によって家具を選べるということはとても大事なことなんです。

嘉門　閲覧席の椅子については、何度もここを訪れたくなるようなバリエーションを用意していただきました。グレートホールは動的な空間だと思うのですが、その中に止まり木のように椅子があちこちに設置されていることは、本と出会う上で非常に効果的です。

窓辺は静的な空間で、館全体としては静と動の空間の妙があるのが建物として面白いところだと思います。窓辺でくつろぎたい時もあれば、歩き回って本と出会いたいと思う時もあるでしょうし、そういった振れ幅を持たせることを意識してきました。

川上　それぞれの場所で、どんな人たちが、どのように滞在するのか。そのための様々なスペースと椅子のあり方を検討しました。ちょっと遊びになるような部分が話題になってもいいだろうし、そんなことをデザインに織り込んでいます。なかなか答えは出ないのですが、様々な利用のシーンを想定し、それぞれに見合ったものを用いた感じです。

色彩については、ベーシックな色味を押さえつつ、それに近いところからバリエーションをつくっていきました。全体的にはフワッとした柔らかな雰囲気を求めていったわけですが、加賀五彩を基調にしたこともあり、アレンジとしてはまとめやすかったかもしれません。"百脚繚乱"のバリエーションをつくるとしても、それぞれの個性を発揮しながら、どのように整合性を取るのかを考えなければなりません。ある種の静けさも必要ですからね。

one is able to pick furniture depending on how you feel.

Kamon: Regarding the reading area chairs, we offered a variation that would make visitors want to keep on returning. As the Great Hall is a dynamic space, the fact that within this, the chairs are planted here and there like perches is a very effective way to encounter books.

The window spaces are static; the library in its entirety has a strange mix of stillness and motion, which is an interesting characteristic. Sometimes, you want to unwind by the window and other times, take a walk and encounter books. We consciously tried to provide for such a big range of motion.

Kawakami: What type of people will in what way spend time in each space? How the various spaces and chairs should be was examined to respond to this. We thought it would be nice to have a bit of a playful element become a topic for conversation, and this is woven into the design. It is difficult to find an answer, but we have visualized various scenes of use and implemented something suited to each.

We kept the basic colors as the main color scheme while creating variations close to those colors. We mainly aimed for a light, gentle atmosphere, and the overall arrangement was probably easy to create because we had already decided on the Kaga-Gosai as base colors.

Even if we made a profusion of chair variations, we would have to consider how to maintain conformity while showing the character of each. There needs to be some sort of serenity, too.

実際に本やモノに触れる価値の再発見

Rediscovering the Value of Physically Touching Books and Objects

嘉門　司書たちの思いを、どのように汲み取っていくかということも重要でした。さきほど川上先生におっしゃっていただいた「本と出会う12のテーマ」を頑張ってつくって、それを動的な部分、グレートホールに配置していったのですが、司書の「本を魅力的に見せたい」という思いを具現化できたのではないかと思います。

川上　それと最近よく言われている「サードプレイス」というか、新しい暮らし方を実現するための場としての意義があると思います。日常における文化的な交流の場としての図書館が、これからますます求められるところでしょうね。

仙田　同じ場所を共有しているという安心感だよね。

Kamon: It was also essential to understand and incorporate the hopes and thoughts of the librarians. We did our best to create the twelve "book encountering" themes that Mr. Kawakami discussed earlier and placed them in the dynamic space of the Great Hall. I think we were able to realize the wishes of the librarians to present the books attractively.

Kawakami: I think the library also has significance as a "third place", as it has frequently been called recently—a place to create and implement new ways of living. More and more, libraries that act as places for cultural interaction in everyday life will be in demand from now on.

Senda: It is the sense of security in sharing the same space.

Kawakami: That's right, shareability. It is becoming increasingly vital,

川上　共有性ですよね。特に最近の若い世代が、個別で情報端末の情報に頼り続けているような状況では、ますます重要になっていますね。

嘉門　この図書館は早くも、県内で最も人が集まる公共施設の一つになりました。この先50年以上を見据えた計画ですから、県民が愛着を持ち続けるようにしたかった。それに家具も含めた総体として魅力的な空間を仕立てることで応えていただいた。新たな風景が生まれ、この地域に厚みがもたらされました。

さらに、一人の人間が小さい時から利用し、高齢者になっても来続けてもらうという、人生全体のスパンで考えようと臨んでもいました。そのためにも「何度来ても、その都度発見がある」と言ってもらえる環境が生まれてよかったと思います。

仙田　もともと、石川県の県立図書館というのが、文化的な交流だけでなく、ディスプレイデザインというか、いわゆる博物館的な要素を重視していました。石川県は伝統文化はもちろん、技術的にも美術的にも蓄積のある土地柄ですからね。

歴史的に図書館は博物館と一体的な施設だったわけですが、今回はその原点に返るようなかたちで、本とモノが同時に訴えかけるような場になったのではないかと思います。これからの図書館には、元々博物館が備えていたような、施設とモノとの関係性が必要なのではないかと考えているのです。

川上　「ディスプレイ」や「展示」「ソフト」が重視される時代になってきたという気がしますね。

仙田　私の事務所でも"こども科学館"や"こども博物館"の設計で展示の領域にも取り組んでいるものだから、そのあたりは意識して作業してきたわけです。今回は川上さんと共にトータルメディア開発研究所の方にも間に入っていただいて、ざっくばらんにいろいろ議論しましたね。展示関係全般について、彼らにうまく調整していただいたと思います。

嘉門　決してデザインをバラバラにしようということではなくて、図書館の中身をどう活かしていくかをじっくり考えていただくべく、トータルメディア開発研究所にお世話になった感じです。

川上　デジタル情報だけではなくて、実物を見たり、触れたりすることができる図書館のあり方を再検討することになりましたね。

仙田　さらに、ニューヨークの図書館の映画（「ニューヨーク公共図書館 エクス・リブリス」、フレデリック・ワイズマン監督、2017年）では、教育現場としての図書館をクローズアップしていました。

川上　それこそデジタル化の中で、いわゆる情報弱者を生まないように、市民に教育の機会を提供したり、就職の斡旋をしたりね。

仙田　市民全体の知的レベルや生活レベルを、いかに上げるかのツールとしても機能しているんですね。

川上　ニューヨーク公共図書館には92の分館があるということなのですが、それが全部リンクしつつ、地域ごとに機能しているんです。9.11のテロがあった時も、一番地元に対して情報を発信していたのは図書館だったと言われています。

仙田　石川県立図書館の立地は、金沢美術工芸大学の新キャンパス

particularly with the current young generation, who tend to rely on information from devices separately.

Kamon: This library has quickly become one of the public buildings where most people gather in the prefecture. Since the project was planned for the next 50 years, we wanted to make sure that the residents would continue to be attached to it. We responded to this by creating an attractive space as a whole, including the furniture. New scenery was brought in and some depth was given to the area.

We also wanted to be thinking in terms of a person's whole life span, coming from a young age to when they continue to use it in old age. In that sense, I am glad that an environment was created where people can go back repeatedly and say "I still make new discoveries on each visit."

Senda: Initially, the Ishikawa prefectural library was intended not only for cultural exchange, but also to focus on display design or "museum-like" components. The reason being that Ishikawa Prefecture has land that has accumulated in terms of traditional culture, certainly, but also in terms of technology and art.

Historically, libraries and museums were combined in one establishment. I believe this design went back to those origins, providing a space where books and objects can simultaneously appeal to and attract visitors. In the future, I think libraries need the type of relationship between building and object that museums used to provide.

Kawakami: I sense that this has become an age where display, exhibition, and software are increasingly emphasized and valued.

Senda: In designing Children's Science Museums and other Children's Museums, my office has engaged with the exhibition design field before, so we were conscious of that while working on this project. This time, working with Mr. Kawakami and the Total Media Development Institute staff, a lot of open discussion was possible. They did very well in coordinating all the exhibition-related aspects.

Kamon: By no means were we trying to separate the design into different parts. So, the Total Media Development Institute was a great help in carefully and deliberately considering how to use the library's contents to the fullest.

Kawakami: It became a re-examination of how libraries should be—not only providing digital information but also creating the opportunity to see and touch real, physical things.

Senda: Furthermore, a film about New York City's library ("Ex Libris: The New York Public Library," directed by Frederick Wiseman, 2017) gave us a close-up look at libraries as educational spaces.

Kawakami: Amid the age of digitalization, we need to offer citizens job-hunting support and educational opportunities to prevent people from becoming so-called "information poor."

Senda: It can also function as a tool for raising the intellectual level and the quality of life of all citizens.

Kawakami: The New York Public Library has 92 satellite libraries, and while they serve their region, they are all linked together. It is said that even during the 9/11 terror attacks, the library delivered the most information locally.

Senda: It is quite significant that Ishikawa Prefectural Library is located adjacent to the new campus of Kanazawa College of Art.

柔らかくて包み込むような
環境、空間でこそ、長く居続けられる（仙田）

と隣接していることが大きいですね。学生が図書館で作品の発表会
をしたり、展示をしたり、様々な利用の可能性が開かれていると思
います。それは図書館と大学のいずれにとっても、また、石川県や
金沢市にとっても望ましいことだと思いますね。

嘉門　ここは元々、金沢大学の土地でしたからね。アカデミックな
エリアだったので、そのコンテクストを受け継ぎつつ、図書館と
美術大学に生まれ変わったわけです。

おかげさまで、この図書館は県民をはじめ多くの方々が気楽に訪れ、
すごく自然なかたちで満喫できる場になりました。館内を歩いて、
気になる本を見つけて、座って読む。実際に足を運んだからこそ
の楽しさや居心地のよさを感じることができる建築になったと思い
ます。私自身も、そんな身体的な体験ができる公共空間のありがた
みをしみじみ感じます。

これからデジタル化がさらに進めば、ますます本というものの価値
が相対的に問われていくことでしょう。だからこそ、人が集まり、
共に時間を過ごし、実際の本に触れるすばらしさを実感できる場所
にしていきたい、していかなければならないと考えています。

2023年1月26日収録

This opens up the possibility for students to use the library in various ways, like presenting works and holding exhibitions. It's beneficial for the library and the university, Ishikawa Prefecture, and Kanazawa City, too.

Kamon: That is because this was formerly Kanazawa University grounds. It was an academic area, so that context was inherited and transformed into a library and art college.

Thanks to everyone's contributions, this library has become a place where a lot of people, beginning with Ishikawa's residents, can freely visit and enjoy themselves. They walk around, find a book, and sit to read. By physically visiting the library, visitors can sense the fun and comfort of the building. Personally, I feel appreciative of a public space that allows for such bodily experiences.

As digitalization progresses further, the relative value of books will be debated even more. All the more reason, we want to, and should, make it a place where people can come together, spend time, and experience the brilliance of really touching books.

Interviewed on January 26, 2023

文化交流エリア2階。学会開催時には右側のパネルにポスター等が貼られる。

3階南の専門開架書架エリア。窓際は半個室的なスペースとなっており、伝統
工芸の展示ケースも設けられている。外の景色を楽しみながら読書ができる。

（上）4階リングから3階のラウンジを見る。

（下左）4階リングの小さなテーブルはとても人気が高い。

（下右）グレートホールの外側、3階の開架スペース。専門的な本を配架するとともに、居心地のよい、隠れ家的な、多様な居場所を設けている。

外壁のパネルとパネルの間にある、隙間的な半個室的な空間。様々な椅子や衝立が設置されている。

3階のブリッジは特別な場所。座り心地がよく、目にも楽しい椅子と触れ合いながら、ゆっくりとファッションやデザインの本を読むことができる。

面陳された書棚とソファ。すぐに手に取って読んでみたくなる。

（上）DVDなど映像ソフトを紹介するディスプレイ棚。
（下）2階のコロシアム型の書棚に向かい合うように、川上元美氏デザインの交互に座れるソファが設置されている。

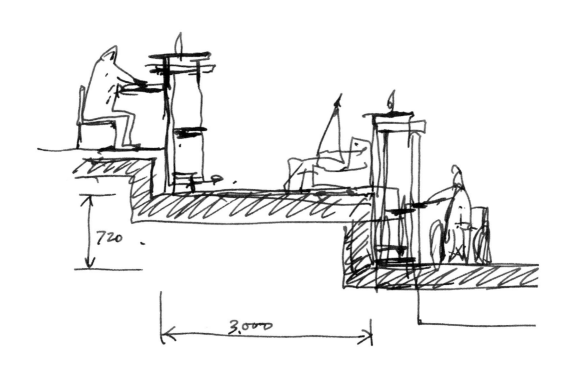

720

3,000

寸法が人の行動を規制する。
又人の行動を発展させる。
若い頃何でもかんでも測り出した。
あの頃の思い出がよみがえる。
3米という寸法の重要性に気づく。

V

Construction Work and Exhibition Design

図書館建築における「演出」とは？

What are "value-adding elements" in library architecture?

水間政典

Masanori MIZUMA

トータルメディア開発研究所
東日本事業部

仙田 満

Mitsuru SENDA

環境デザイン研究所会長

池畑木綿子

Yuko IKEHATA

石川県立図書館 司書専門員
※建設当時：文化振興課新図書館整備推進室

塩津淳司

Junji SHIOTSU

トータルメディア開発研究所
東日本事業部

矢尾志津江

Shizue YAO

石川県土木部営繕課課長補佐
※建設当時

優れた図書館には、ハード面における卓越した技術と共に、演出・ソフト面での様々な工夫が注ぎ込まれている。
本館の建築工事と展示設計の現場において中心的な役割を果たした人々が一堂に会して、
いかにして本館の魅力をつくり出そうとしたのか、未来を見据えた思いのたけも含めて活発な意見交換を行った。

A good library integrates mixed innovative approaches for its presentation and intangible elements, as well as outstanding technologies for its tangible elements. The key players in the main building construction and exhibition design had a lively discussion about their efforts to make the main building attractive, and their future outlook.

身体を動かす、新しい図書館像
A New Library Integrating Physical Actions

仙田　この本の座談会で何度かお話ししているのですが、私は昔、広島市民球場を設計して、協働した市の営繕課の方が今、区長になっているんです。その方から中国新聞にこんなコラム記事が出ていたと知らせてくれたんです。

それは今、広島に住んでいる方が、かつて金沢にも住んでいたことがあって、しばらくぶりに金沢を訪れて、石川県立図書館に入ったら、非常に感激した。本を探すというよりも好奇心の海を泳ぐように歩き回ったと。そのコメントは利用者の目線から、この図書館の特徴を言い当てているなと思ったんです。

今、広島でも市立図書館が駅ビルの中に移転するという計画が話題になっているのですが、そのコラムは広島でも市民の誇りとなるような図書館をつくってほしいという風に結んでありました。

この石川県立図書館では、来館者の好奇心を掻き立てるような様々な建築的、あるいは展示的な仕掛けを施すことができたのではないかと思います。面陳のような本の並べ方や配置なども含めて、様々な工夫を皆さんのおかげで凝らすことができました。

プロポーザルの際には、公園のような図書館をつくりたいという提案をしたのですが、当初から従来の図書館の概念を超えて、いわゆる文化交流というか、地域の文化に触れながら、知的好奇心をいかに育んでいけるかということが、コンセプトの核になっていたと思います。

池畑　ひと昔前からMLA（ミュージアム・ライブラリー・アーカイブス）の連携ということが言われていますが、もはや情報を得るという意味では、それらの間の壁がなくなってきています。人が知的情報を得る手段の一つが読書になりますが、わざわざ図書館を訪れることに、どのような意義を込められるのか。

例えばここでは、広い館内において、来館者にわかりやすいように、従来型の図書の分類だけではなく、人の生活に寄り添ったテーマを設けて配架を行い、歩いて情報を得るということがしやすくなるような仕掛けを施しています。さらに歩き回ってインプットした情報を、文化交流エリアでアウトプットするなど、インプットとアウトプットの両方が可能になっているわけです。このように身体を動かして情報に触れる、体感するということが、これからの図書館の意義になるのではないかと考えています。

仙田　もともと図書館という施設は、歴史的に見ても大きな意味で博物館ですよね。博物館への原点回帰という意味でも、石川県立図書館では地域の文化や風土などを含めた、様々な要素を配架や展示によって表現しようとしています。

本来、図書館や美術館、水族館も博物館の範疇にあったのですが、それが近代化と共にどんどん分かれてきてしまったわけです。今、それらが改めて融合しようとしているのは、一つの時代の方向性ではないかと思いますね。

矢尾　基本構想の段階から「文化」というキーワードを掲げていまし

Senda: I've already mentioned this in the roundtable discussions for this book several times, but when I designed the Hiroshima Municipal Stadium, I worked with a person from the city's maintenance department who is now a ward mayor. He mentioned an article in the Chugoku Shimbun.

It was about a message from a person living in Hiroshima who used to live in Kanazawa. When this person visited the Ishikawa Prefectural Library in Kanazawa for the first time in a while, they were extremely impressed—it was as if swimming in a sea of curiosity rather than looking for books. It describes the very nature of the library from a user's point of view.

Hiroshima City is currently discussing a plan to relocate its library to the station building, and the article concluded with a request to build a library that the citizens of Hiroshima will be proud of.

I believe the Ishikawa Prefectural Library successfully incorporated a variety of architectural and exhibit features to arouse users' curiosity. Thanks to everyone's help, various ideas were employed, including the arrangement and layout of the books to have a face-out display.

We suggested a park-like library in our proposal. From the very beginning, the core of our concept was the cultivation of intellectual curiosity while learning about local culture, or "cultural exchange," beyond the conventional concept of a library.

Ikehata: It's been a while since people started talking about the concept of MLA (Museums, Libraries, and Archives), but their boundaries no longer exist in terms of information acquisition. Reading is one way of obtaining intellectual information, but what kind of significance can we find in physically visiting a library?

For example, this library arranges books by themes relevant to people's lives, in addition to conventional book categories, so that users can easily access information in the large library. Furthermore, the cultural exchange area allows users to output the information they obtained by walking around, enabling them to both input and output information. I believe that the significance of libraries of the future lies in physical actions like these to experience and access information.

Senda: Historically, libraries can be considered as museums in the broad sense. To return to this starting point, the Ishikawa Prefectural Library is trying to communicate various features, including local culture and climate, through its shelf arrangement and exhibits.

Libraries, art museums, and aquariums were originally categorized as museums, but modernization caused subdivisions. I think that the current trend is directed toward their fusion once again.

Yao: "Culture" has been a keyword since the idea conception phase, but it was initially unclear how it would relate to both tangible and intangible elements. This time, we built and connected each of these areas while working with the New Library Development Promotion Office and Mr. Senda from the design phase.

「文化」をテーマにハードとソフトを構築し
繋ぎ合わせる作業を行った（矢尾）

たが、ハード的にもソフト的にも、どのように関連づけていくのか、当初はぼんやりしていたように思います。今回は新図書館整備推進室や仙田先生と設計段階からご一緒しながら、それぞれを構築して、繋ぎ合わせる作業をしてまいりました。

仙田　私がプロポーザルの時に出した案では、図書の領域と、文化交流の領域という2核による構成だったんです。その後、それらを混ぜるというか、相互に組み合わせるような作業を経て1核になったわけですが、それが奏功したのではないかと考えています。

今回、トータルメディア開発研究所の皆さんには、展示という領域でご協力いただいたわけですが、手応えはいかがですか。

水間　「文化交流」というテーマへの取り組みについては、おそらく我々が最後のワンピースになったのだと思います。コンセプトも建築設計も固まってきて、どのような展示を行うかという部分で、当社を指名していただいたわけです。推進室の方々のビジョンも受けて、文化交流のあり方とともに、それをどのようにかたちにするかという部分に関わらせていただいたものと思います。

当社も普段は博物館などをメインに活動しており、図書館に関わる機会がほとんどないという状況でリサーチを行い、先ほどから伺っているような、図書館のあり方が変わりつつあるという状況を理解しました。そして、石川県の様々な施策の中で、この図書館が「文化交流」をテーマにしたことの意味をよく理解することができました。その中で、先ほど池畑さんがおっしゃった、静的な図書館という本を読むだけの場から、動きのある、新しい図書館像にはまる展示とは何だろうかというのを考えました。結果的に展示の可能性を広げ、新たな発見をもたらすようなプロジェクトになりましたね。

矢尾　図書館における展示って何だろう？と、何度も自問自答しました（笑）

Senda: My suggestion in the proposal consisted of two cores: a reading zone and a cultural exchange zone. Later, they were combined into a single core by mixing, or rather, alternating them, and I think it was a success.

The Total Media Development Institute participated in this project in the exhibit development. What is your take on it?

Mizuma: We were probably the last piece of the puzzle in tackling the theme of cultural exchange. Our company was appointed when the concept and architectural design had been finalized, and the next step was to detail the exhibits. We worked on determining a cultural exchange approach and how to put it into practice, while taking into account the vision of the Promotion Office.

Our company's primary clients are museums, and we had little experience working with libraries. So we did some research and learned about the changing situation around libraries that you mentioned earlier. This helped us to better understand why "cultural exchange" is the theme of this library, among the various other policies of Ishikawa Prefecture.

In the process, we sought for exhibits befitting the image of a new dynamic library, different from a static library just for reading books like Ms. Ikehata mentioned earlier. The project turned out to expand the possibilities of the exhibits and brought about new findings.

Yao: I often asked myself, "What exactly is an exhibition in a library?" (laughs).

図書スペースに展示を取り込む

Incorporating Exhibitions into a Reading Space

仙田　私が好きな本で小説家の松浦寿輝さんが書いた『知の庭園』という本があります。「19世紀パリの空間装置」という副題がついているのですが、図書館について触れているんです。この本で彼が図書館の原点として取り上げているのが大英博物館のリーディングルームなんですよ。それはすなわち図書館なのですが、大英博物館の中心にあるんです。要するに博物館の中に図書館がしっかり据えられているんですね。

石川県立図書館ではそれを逆にして、図書館の中に展示的な要素を持ち込んでいます。図書スペースの中に工芸品を展示するなど、様々なかたちで文化的なプロダクトを取り入れているというのは、図書館のあり方として世界的にも新しいのではないでしょうか。

水間　普通は図書スペースと展示のスペースを分類、区別しますよね。でも、ここではそれが融合していて非常に面白いですね。

仙田　玄関を入ったところで石川の文化や自然についての展示を打ち出して（里の恵み・文化の香り〜石川コレクション〜）、そこからスロープで上がっていくという。そのかたちは基本設計の段階から温めてきました。さらに2階でも、本とプロダクトが融合するかたちで「石川県立自然史資料館コーナー」を設けるなど、様々な実験的な試みを行いました。

塩津　「文化交流」というテーマが図面に書かれているのを見た時、交流ということは行き来がある、しかもそれは強制的なものではないと理解しました。それが図書館という静的な場所で実現するのかと心配していたのですが、実際にオープンしてみると、本当にうまく機能しているなと思いますね。

仙田　ラボ機能（モノづくり体験スペース）も取り込みましたね。やはり本と共にものづくり、あるいは体験的なものとが融合しないと、うまく知が循環していかないのではないか、という気がしているんです。軽井沢に2020年に開校した風越学園という新しい教育コンセプトを掲げている学校を設計したのですが、そこでも図書室をベースにして、理科や工作、音楽など、モノづくりや発表を行うような教室を並べたんです。モノをつくって、発表して、それに触れたら、図書室ですぐに調べて、さらに庭で実験をしたり、そんな連携を可能にした学校です。

Senda: One of my favorite books is *Chi No Teien (The Garden of Knowledge)* by novelist Hisaki Matsuura. With a subtitle meaning *"spatial devices of 19th century Paris"* in English, it contains descriptions of libraries. In this book, he insists that the Reading Room of the British Museum was the starting point of libraries. The Reading Room is indeed a library, located in the center of the British Museum—in short, a library placed within a museum.

The Ishikawa Prefectural Library flipped this around and introduced exhibition features into the library. It incorporates cultural materials using various approaches, such as displaying handicrafts in the library. I think this is probably new to libraries around the world.

Mizuma: Spaces for books and exhibitions are usually separated. But this library combines both, which is really interesting.

Senda: Ishikawa's culture- and nature-related materials (Ishikawa Collection) are exhibited at the entrance, which connects to an ascending slope. This was incubated since the schematic design. The second floor also integrated various experimental ideas, such as the Ishikawa Museum of Natural History Space which involves both books and products.

Shiotsu: When I saw the theme of "cultural exchange" written on the plans, I realized that exchange means interactions that are not forced. I was a little skeptical if this would be possible in a static place like a library, but after its opening, I think it's working really well.

Senda: The Makers Workspace that functions as a laboratory was also introduced. I think that a knowledge cycle doesn't work well unless books are combined with creative activities or hands-on experiences.

I designed the Karuizawa Kazakoshi School, which opened in 2020, with a new educational concept. Its design is also centered around a library, accompanied by classrooms for creative activities and presentations such as science, crafts, and music. The school enables a chain of actions: creating things and presenting them, looking for more information about them in the library right away, and conducting more experiments in the schoolyard.

面陳とスロープを取り入れた閲覧エリア

Main Library Area with Face-out Display and Slopes

仙田　でもやっぱり、多くの人がこの図書館のグレートホールにおける本の並べ方、面陳という手法に感心しているんですよね。

池畑　表紙が見えるように置く「面陳列」を"面陳"と呼んでいます。今の時代、インターネットでも本はまず、表紙で目にしますよね。現実をネットと同じにする必要はないのですが、何が本にアプローチするきっかけになるのかを考えると、ネットに慣れてきた世代の人にとっては、背表紙が並んでいるよりも、そういうかたちの方が選びやすいんですね。普段、あまり本を読まない人にとっても、手に取りやすいということかもしれません。

仙田　それに加えて、矢尾さんと一緒に取り組んだ、車椅子を念頭に置いたスロープのスケール感の検討が大きいですね。約3mの幅の中に車椅子や閲覧机、ソファなどを配置することを想定し、多様な人々が興味を抱いた時にすぐ手に取って、そこで読めるという状況を構築したわけです。

矢尾　やはり県の施設として整備するということで、誰もが安心して使えるということは必須条件ですし、今回は障がいのある方にもご協力いただきました。仙田先生には設計の初期の頃に、県立の特別支援学校に一緒に行っていただいて、想定したスロープと同じ勾配があるところで、実際に車椅子に乗って、動いて、体感していただきましたね。

仙田　広島球場でもここの1/15勾配に近い200mのスロープを提案したんですよ。広島駅の方から球場へ向かうアプローチが、スロープを設置するのにちょうどいい寸法だったんですね。実際に障がい者の方々の観戦が増えたということで、スロープの効果を実感したものです。

矢尾　今回は閲覧エリアにスロープを設けたわけですが、当初、司書さんからはブックトラックはスロープで停車できるのか、という声が上がりました。バリアフリーの基準上、スロープを設けると両側に手すりが必要になるし、書架のところではどうするのか、といったことについて一つひとつ実験、体験しながらクリアしてきました。例えば、手すりを書架側に設けると邪魔にならないかという心配があったのですが、四肢麻痺などで手の力が弱い人は、そこを仮置き場のスペースとして使用できることが検証でわかったりして、実際にいろいろと工夫しながら進めていきましたね。

仙田　少しずつ試していきましたね。日本図書館協会理事長の植松(貞夫)さんも、スロープが図書館に入り込んだ事例は世界にも珍しいと言っていますし、結果的にスロープの3mという幅はうまくいったのではないかと思います。

矢尾　あの幅も広ければいいというものでもなくて、本を手に取るスペースとソファ、その間を通過するスペースなどを考慮して検討を進めたわけです。変に間延びせず、それでも使いやすいという幅の設定は難しかったですね。

Senda: In the end, many people are impressed with how the books are displayed—known as the face-out display—in the Central Atrium of the library.

Ikehata: The arrangement where book covers are facing outward is called "face-out display." In this digital age, the first encounter with a book online often involves a book cover. It's not necessary to recreate the situation in reality, but considering what intrigues potential readers, the face-out display helps to make books more enticing for digital natives, rather than lined-up spines. Like this, even for reluctant readers, it's probably easier to pick a book.

Senda: Another key was determining the dimensions of the wheelchair-accessible slope, which I worked on with Ms. Yao. The approximately 3m-wide slope was designed to be wide enough for wheelchairs, as well as arranging reading desks and sofas. It's a space where various people can get a book of their interest and read it right there.

Yao: As a prefectural facility, being accessible to everyone is an essential requirement, so we asked for the cooperation of people with disabilities for this project. Mr. Senda and I visited a prefectural special needs school in the early design phase, and we actually tested a wheelchair on a slope with the same gradient as our plan.

Senda: I proposed a 200m slope with a similar 1/15 gradient for the Hiroshima stadium as well. The approach from Hiroshima Station to the stadium had the perfect dimensions for a slope. I heard that more people with disabilities come to games, and this made me realize the effect of the slope.

Yao: For this library, the slope was incorporated in the Main Library Area. At first, some librarians asked if a book truck could be parked on the slope. A slope would require handrails on both sides to meet the barrier-free design standards, and they asked about our plan around the bookshelves. We solved each problem by testing and trying.

For instance, there was a concern that handrails in front of bookshelves might get in people's way. But it turned out that the handrails could be used by people with weak hands, such as people with quadriplegia, to temporarily place books. We worked through various creative ideas.

Senda: We tried things little by little. The Japan Library Association's president (Sadao) Uematsu said that an integrated slope in a library is a rare case in the world. I think the 3m width worked out well.

Yao: It wasn't like the wider, the better. The width was determined after considering the necessary areas for browsing books and placing sofas while leaving enough room to pass by. It was difficult to find a width that would not be excessively roomy, but still be user-friendly.

石川県の文化・自然を解釈する

Interpreting the Culture and Nature of Ishikawa Prefecture

仙田　展示に関しては、たくさんの人間国宝を擁している「石川県の文化」に加えて、「自然環境」がもう一つ、大きなテーマになりました。いろいろ試行錯誤したのですが、どういうところに苦労がありましたか。

水間　博物館であれば通常、コンテンツを来館者に伝えるためのコミュニケーションの仕組みをつくっていくのですが、図書館の場合、来館者が求めるものが様々ですし、展示される自然についての情報もどんどん変わっていくので、こういう仕組みをつくれば完成、ということにはなりませんでした。

まずは司書の方々がどんな業務をしているのかを把握するところから始めて、文化立県石川の自然とは何なのかということを理解した上で、展示の仕組みや装置がどのように成立するのか、ということを検討しました。

一般的な博物館、ミュージアムであれば、実際の自然の造形を館内につくろう、という発想が出てきたりするのですが（笑）。今回は「自然」についての本を、司書さんが展示用に再構成されたりしているので、それに対応できる器をつくりました。司書さんたちが整理された本やプロダクト、様々な情報との繋がりをつくる結節点となり、来館者に興味を持って見ていただくための装置を必死に考え

Senda: As for the exhibits, the natural environment was selected as a major theme, in addition to the culture of Ishikawa Prefecture, which is home to many "living national treasures." There were many trials and errors. What was the difficult part?

Mizuma: For a museum, we usually develop a system to communicate the displayed content to visitors, but for a library, visitors' expectations vary, and the displayed information of the natural environment constantly changes. So it wasn't like we could develop a certain system and be done.

We started by understanding the work of librarians, and the natural environment of a culture-driven Ishikawa Prefecture. With this insight, we explored how to establish an exhibition structure and mechanism.

For a typical museum, we might suggest recreating the natural environment inside the museum (laughs). But for this project, the librarians reorganize nature-themed books for display, so we created a framework to accommodate such exhibits. We strove to develop a mechanism that would entice visitors and serve as a node to link books, products, and various information organized by the librarians. I think it was a very different approach from our previously designed exhibitions.

Shiotsu: Since its nature as the "library of Ishikawa Prefecture" had to be emphasized, people from Tokyo like us couldn't just design it easily. So,

たという感じですね。今までの展示のつくり方とは、だいぶ違うアプローチになったと思います。

塩津　本当に「石川県の図書館」という性格が強いので、東京者の我々が簡単につくれるものではないというところで、とにかくリサーチや検証を重ねました。

水間　石川の自然とは何かを考えると、文化と自然の連動性があるというのが特徴ではないか。例えば里山が単体で成立しているのではなく、文化によって自然が生み出され、そこからまた文化が生まれている。ある種の日本的な文化のあり方のすばらしさだと思うのですが、そういったところを理解した上でわかりやすく展示できる仕組みを考えていきました。

仙田　建築についても、いかに石川の文化・自然を解釈していくのかということを、皆さんと議論しながら進めていきましたね。中でもラメラドームの天井をブルーに設定したことについては、成巽閣の「群青の間」から引用したと説明したわけですが、これが実現できたことに私は本当に感謝しているんですよ。

矢尾　あの色を決めるタイミングというのは、現場で足場を組んで、もう塗装しようという直前だったんです。先生が現場に来られて、試し塗りしたのを見て、「わりかし、いいな」と言われて、設計時のパースとは全く違う色だったので、どうしようかと（笑）

池畑　たくさんの来館者があの青いのがいいと言って、天井の写真を撮っていますね。結果的に行政としても英断だったのではないかと思います。

仙田　この図書館を前田家との歴史的な繋がりの中で考えていただく、きっかけにもなったのではないかと思います。

we did a lot of research and verification.

Mizuma: When thinking about Ishikawa's natural environment, it can be characterized by the bond between the culture and nature. It's not like the "Satoyama"-like environment exists independently, but instead, the culture nurtures the nature, which again nurtures the culture. I think this is the beauty of a certain kind of Japanese culture. We pursued an accessible exhibition system that takes into account such understanding.

Senda: Discussion about the architectural design also involved how to interpret Ishikawa's culture and nature. I'm particularly grateful that we could make the ceiling of the lamella dome blue, which I explained was derived from the Ultramarine Room of Seisonkaku (villa of the Maeda family, the former lord of the area).

Yao: The color was determined when the scaffolding was already in place and painting was about to begin. Mr. Senda visited the site and saw the test-painted part, and said, "I like it better than I thought." It was completely different from the design perspective image, so there was a bit of confusion (laughs).

Ikehata: We see many visitors taking pictures of the ceiling, saying they like the blue color. I think the government made a wise decision.

Senda: I think it offers a good opportunity for people to view this library in the context of its historical connection with the Maeda family.

Shiotsu: I was really surprised to see the ceiling painted blue when the building was still under construction with exposed concrete, and there were no books or anything yet.

Ikehata: Mr. Senda foresaw the final building with all the components in place, didn't you? Not many people can envision that far.

Shiotsu: When the books were finally displayed face-out with a flood of color, they somehow resonated with the ceiling color. Before the books

文化と自然の連動性があるという
石川県の特徴をわかりやすく提案（水間）

塩津　建設中、まだ本も何もない、コンクリートも打ちっ放しの状態で、天井が青色に塗られた時は本当にびっくりしました。

池畑　先生は最終的に全部の要素が入った時のことまで、考えられていたわけですよね。普通の人はそこまで、なかなか想像できないです。

塩津　最後に本が面陳で並べられて、色がバーッと入った時に、天井の色と響き合うものがありましたね。本が入るまではもう、ドキドキしていました（笑）

仙田　さらに廣村（正彰）さんに手がけていただいたサインも、大きな目次のように12の項目を表していて、新しい試みとして注目されていますね。

矢尾　サインについても、先生に途中、何度も相談しましたね。県の内部からは、今回の建物はいわゆる1階、2階、3階という単純な階層で区切られていないので、来館者にわかりにくいんじゃないか、ということを常に言われていたわけです。

従来の図書館では、目的の本にどれだけスムーズにたどり着くかということが重視されていて、県内部でもそのイメージが強かったのですが、今回はそれ以外の側面もあって、「公園のようにめぐって、新しい知識と出会う」ということもテーマになっているんです、ということを伝えつつ、この広くて複雑な館内をどのように案内するのか、というのが大きな課題としてありました。

その時にこちらから、石川県には加賀五彩というものがあるから、活用できたらいいなという思いもお伝えしました。廣村先生が書架の上にテーマを表す言葉をドンと置かれた時に「あ、なるほど」と思ったんですね。いわゆるサインの機能だけでなく、空間の中に締まりを与えてくれたので、シンプルにすごいなと思いました。

また、照明についても、本を読むところだから、とにかく明るくという意見がある中で、どれだけ演出的な要素を併せ持たせることが

came in, I felt so nervous (laughs).

Senda: The signs designed by Mr. (Masaaki) Hiromura display 12 headings, like a table of contents. This new idea is also attracting attention.

Yao: We consulted with you about the signs many times as well. The prefectural government had repeatedly pointed out that the visitors might find it hard to navigate, because the building was not simply zoned by level, like first, second, and third levels.

Conventional libraries place emphasis on how easily visitors can find books they are looking for, and this was important for the prefecture as well. So we explained that this library has other aspects, and one of its themes is "a place to walk around like in a park and encounter new knowledge." One of our major issues was how to navigate visitors through this large and complex library.

At that time, we also explained that we'd like to use Ishikawa Prefecture's traditional Kaga-Gosai colors (five colors of Kaga textiles). When Mr. Hiromura placed text describing the theme on a bookshelf, I thought, "Wow, I see." I thought it was simply genius, because it not only served as a sign but also livened up the room.

As for the lighting, some insisted on making it as bright as possible for reading, but we requested to also include elements that would enhance the ambiance. Setting the color temperature was another challenge. When the building was completed, we were pleased to hear comments that it didn't feel dark.

できるかというところで希望を言わせていただきました。色温度の設定もなかなか難しかったのですが、実際にでき上がってみて、暗い印象はないという評価もいただけたので、よかったと思います。

訪れるたびに、新たな発見を楽しんで
New Discoveries to Enjoy Every Visit

池畑　先ほど大英博物館のお話をされていましたが、やはり、ここの図書館の基本は図書であり、しっかりしたレファレンスコーナーもあるという風に、ネット世代の方にも図書の情報の確かさや、そこから調べていくメリットを実感していただければと思います。

その上で博物館や美術館の学芸員にお越しいただいて、昆虫標本をつくったり、歴史や美術について教えてもらったり、といったイベントも行っています。普段から学芸員の方は当館の蔵書を調べに来られますし、逆に我々が展示を行う際にはアドバイスをいただくような連携をとっています。

「石川コレクション」について言えば、県のいろいろな部署から、里山や森林、漁業など、様々な知見をいただいて展示を行っています。一般的な博物館との違いとしては、ガラスケースに入れず、直接触れられるようなかたちでの展示も行っているということが挙げられますね。

県が行っている事業について、直接県民の方々にご説明するようなイベントも行い、それに対応するような展示を手がけるという役割も充実させていきたいですね。

仙田　イベントを結構、活発に行っていますよね。それに合わせて展示にも変化を加えているということですね。

水間　先ほど池畑さんがおっしゃったように、ここの図書館はただ、本を借りに来る場所ではなくて、思いもよらない出会いや、好奇心を刺激するきっかけになるようなことを意図しているわけです。県の方々も好奇心や行動の連続性についてのビジョンを持っておられたので、展示の方でも、そのきっかけとなる入口をつくることを意識しました。

我々としては、来館者の方々がどういう行動を起こす可能性があるのか、そのためのデザインはどうあるべきなのかということをよく考えることになりました。展示であれば、司書さんたちがこういう風につくって、こういう出会いができるとか。ファブラボであれば、こういう機器があって、それらでつくったモノを来館者が見て、つくりたくなる。そこから、また本に繋がっていくというような動きをどんどんつくっていくことが、ここで求められている図書館像だと思います。

Ikehata: You mentioned the British Museum earlier, but the foundation of a library is books, and so we have an extensive reference section. We hope that we can convey to the digital natives the reliability of books as an information source, and the merit of starting research with a book review.

With this in mind, we hold events with invited museum and art curators, such as insect specimen-making classes and history and art lectures. We work closely with curators—they regularly visit the library to look for reference books, and we ask for their advice when planning exhibitions. As for the Ishikawa Collection, we consult with various prefectural departments to gain insights into satoyama, forests, fisheries, and other areas for our exhibits. What distinguishes our exhibits from those in a typical museum is that ours are not behind glass cases, and visitors can touch them directly.

We'd also like to play a more active role in communicating the public works of the prefectural government by holding events to introduce the works in person and creating corresponding exhibits.

Senda: The library is quite active in holding events. And so, the exhibits are modified to coincide with the events, right?

Mizuma: As Ms. Ikehata mentioned earlier, this library is not just a place to visit for books, but is intended to be a place that evokes unexpected encounters and curiosity. The prefectural government also wished for continuous curiosity and movement, so we tried to develop exhibits that would be an entry point to lead to this.

For our part, we had to contemplate visitors' possible actions and the designs required for them. In the case of an exhibit, librarians would plan certain things and it would evoke certain encounters. In the case of a fab lab, there would be certain equipment, and visitors' creativity would be inspired by seeing the products made with the equipment. These would in turn lead to books, resulting in a further expansion of networks. I think this is the ideal that is being sought after for a library.

Shiotsu: We thought that since people come to a library with a certain curiosity or purpose to know or find out something to begin with, it would probably be easy to naturally prompt them to absorb information from exhibits.

The exhibits invite people to the library, and people find their favorite place to spend time, and start to dig deep into themselves. I saw kids

塩津　そもそも図書館という場所は、来館者が何かを知りたい、探したいという好奇心や目的を持って訪れているので、その延長で展示からも情報を吸収しようとすんなり関わっていただけると考えていました。展示も一つのきっかけにして、図書館に入り込んで、それぞれの居場所を見つけて、過ごすというところに繋がり、自分を深めていく作業が始まっていくのかなと。先ほどもスロープのところで、こどもたちが座って本を読んでいる姿を見かけたのですが、どこでも、その人の居場所になる、そういう図書館だと思います。

矢尾　ここに住みたいというご意見もいただいていますね。私の友人も、そう言っていました(笑)

池畑　すごく、うれしいですね。私がここで働いていてよかったなと思うのは、「おしゃべりOK」にしたことで、お子さん連れの方が圧倒的に増えたことです。もともと図書館には一定数の親子連れのヘビーユーザーがいるのですが、それでも一部に過ぎず、こどもが騒ぐから行きにくいという風に遠慮される方もたくさんいたんですね。こどもの立場で考えても、シーッて言われると楽しくなくなるじゃないですか(笑)。だから、こども心にも図書館って楽しいところだな、というイメージを持ってもらえるのが一番いいと思うんですよね。そして、親子のコミュニケーションが充実することが何よりです。
もう一つ、うれしい話としては、あるプロダクトデザイナーの方が、ここの図書館で仕事をしていると言うんですよ。事務所で作業するよりも、ここでやった方がアイデアが湧くからと。ハッと何かを思いついた時に、美術やデザインに限らず、様々な本を取りに行くことができますし、そういう風に使われたらいいなと思っていたので感激しました。

sitting and reading books on the slope earlier, and I thought, this is a library in which everyone can find their place anywhere.

Yao: Some people even say they'd like to live here. One of my friends said the same thing (laughs).

Ikehata: I'm very happy to hear that. What I like about working here is that we've seen a dramatic increase in the number of visitors who bring children, because the library allows talking. The library has always had a certain number of heavy users who bring their kids, but it was still only a small percentage. There are many people who hesitate to visit because kids might be too loud.

If you were a kid, it would be no fun to be told to be quiet (laughs). So, I think it's best if we can give children the impression that the library is a fun place to visit. Improving communication between parents and children is the best thing.

Another story that made me happy is that a product designer uses the library to work because it's more inspiring to get ideas than working in the office. Whenever something comes to mind, a variety of books, not just art and design, are there for reference. I was thrilled to hear this because I was hoping people would use the library in such a way.

Mizuma: One of the project goals was to create exhibits that would attract visitors every time, no matter how many times they've visited. It wasn't an easy task, but we tackled it while having study sessions with the librarians. We also collaboratively developed a system for updating the exhibits and successfully incorporated seasonal changes. So I hope visitors will enjoy discovering something different each time they visit.

Yao: It would be great if people would visit the library many times and find their favorite places, and find new uses for the library, their own ways of using the library. We have a wide variety of places to read, so I'm

来館者の好奇心を掻き立てる様々な建築的・展示的な仕掛けを施すことができた(仙田)

水間　今回は何度来ても、見てもらえるような展示というのが、一つの目標だったんですよ。なかなか難しいお題だったのですが、司書の方々と勉強会みたいなことも行いながら取り組んできました。展示の更新の仕組みなども一緒に構築し、春夏秋冬など時期によって変化のある場所をつくることができたと思っておりますので、訪れるたびに異なる発見をして、楽しんでいただきたいですね。

矢尾　やっぱり何回も足を運んでいただいて、自分のお気に入りの場所を見つけていただく、そして、新しい図書館の使い方というか、自分なりの使い方を開拓していただけたらいいですね。多種多様な閲覧席を設けていますので、いろいろ使っていただけると、必ず新たな発見があると思います。

池畑　仙田先生の「公園のような図書館」という言葉に象徴されるのですが、まずできるだけ多くの方にとって居心地がよい空間であることが求められます。ここをフラッと訪れて、結果的に一冊も読まなかったという方がいても、全然いいと思うんですよ。

ただ、蔵書構築はしっかりしておかなければいけないということは意識しています。何も読まなかったな、という日があってもいいけれども、ふっと好奇心に触れる何かに思い当たって、いざ、調べてみたら、すごい、ここまで調べられるんだ、という風に感じていただけるようにしておきたいなと。

例えば私たちもカウンターや事務室の業務だけでなく、毎日必ずフロアワークを行っていて、全員が円形の棚を分割して担当しています。面陳についても、一日に何度も整えなければならないわけです。そんな中で来館者のお話を伺ったり、反応を見たりしながら、一緒に成長していけたらいいですね。

2023年6月9日収録

---

sure visitors will find something new by using them.

Ikehata: Just like Mr. Senda's description of a "library like a park," a library should be a comfortable place for as many people as possible. It's perfectly fine to visit the library aimlessly and leave without reading a single book.

However, we are well aware of the need to build an excellent book collection. It's OK to visit here and end up reading nothing, but we want to be prepared for situations, like something suddenly intriguing your curiosity and you wanting to look it up. We want you to be amazed by how far you can dig into things with our books.

For example, our routine work includes different tasks in the library area, in addition to those at the counter and in the office. Everyone is responsible for some portion of the circular shelves. The face-out display needs to be tidied up several times a day. While doing this, we'd like to grow together with the visitors by listening to them and seeing their responses.

Interviewed on June 9, 2023

グレートホール1階の閲覧エリアにて。

1階の閲覧エリアに設けられた「石川コレクション」。石川県の自然や文化を紹介するコーナーとなっており、県民はもちろん県外から訪れた人にも、地域の可能性を伝える場所となっている。

（上）"アナログ目次"としての書架上のサイン。
（下）"デジタル目次"としての文化交流エリア1階のブックリウム。

本と文化財の共存。そして何よりも回遊。

石川県立図書館の蔵書へのデジタルなアクセスを可能にする
セルフステーション。

（上）グレートホールに配置された動詞のサインと面陳された本。書架の手すりは、
　　　車いす利用者や高齢者が容易に本を手に取ることができるように、水平で頑丈に設えている。
（下）立体的に構成されたこどもエリア。大人は読書に励み、こどもたちは動き回る。

金沢大学キャンパス時代に
植えられたサクラを保全：
最大限の保存（移植）と、
世代交代のための新植（多種化）
　　　　　　　　　柿ヤ原、傳史

VI
Architecture and Forest

母屋／外壁／ランドスケープのトータルデザインとは？
What is a total design for a building, exterior, and landscape?

柳原博史
Hiroshi YANAGIHARA

ランドスケープアーキテクト
マインドスケープ代表

仙田 満
Mitsuru SENDA

環境デザイン研究所会長

清水貞博
Sadahiro SHIMIZU

atelier A5 建築設計事務所
代表取締役

石川県立図書館を訪れる人々を迎え入れるための演出と言えるのが、
外装やランドスケープといった屋外のデザインだ。
本館では建物に近づくにつれて、様々な色や形が見えてくるような工夫が凝らされている。
さらに屋外と屋内を循環するように歩き回ることで様々な楽しみ方ができる、その魅力について話を聞いた。

The building façade and landscape of the Ishikawa Prefectural Library is designed to welcome visitors to the library.
As visitors approach the main building, they are greeted by an array of colors and shapes.
Moreover, they can enjoy various ways of walking around as if they were cycling between outdoors and indoors.
The three discuss these entrancing features of the place.

大学跡地のランドスケープに求められること

Expectations of a Landscape in a Former University Site

仙田　ここは元々、金沢大学工学部の跡地でした。プロポーザルの時にこの敷地を見たのですが、学校だったということで既存の樹木としてはサクラが多かったんです。それと周辺が住宅地ということもあって、建物は真ん中につくろうと思いました。

できるだけ建物の周囲に緑を残し、駐車場も図書館を囲むように配置していこうと。そうすると、必然的に入口も建物を囲むようなかたちで、あちこちにあるということになったわけですが、柳原さんはこの敷地については、どういう風に見ておられましたか？

柳原　私が初めて訪れた時には、すでに昔の校舎は全部なくなっていましたが、キャンパスの道路線形が残っていましたね。

一つ、考えたのが、隣の神社（上野八幡神社）との関係です。この神社にこんもりとした緑のボリュームがあって、それがすごく目を引いたんです。それ以外はほぼ住宅地なのですが、この緑との関係をどう築くかというのが、ポイントになるだろうと思いました。

それと金沢大学の本館前に車回しとその中央の植栽帯が残されていて、植栽帯の中に何本かの樹木も残されていました。その中で一際目を引いた一本が今、図書館の正面に植わっているアカマツのタギョウショウ（多行松）というすごく立派なものですね。この木は兼六園にもたくさん植えられているのですが、しっかりと仕立てられていて、形もよかったので、これはぜひ残したいなと最初の時点で考えていました。

さらに外側に植わっているサクラも残した方がいいだろうと。既存の木にはボリュームがありますし、新しく植える木とは全然風格が違いますから、絶対残すべきだろうと思いました。

このように真ん中に図書館があって、そのまわりを囲むように大木があるという関係性、放射状に連なっていくような構造は当初からスッとイメージができていました。それに神社との関係性が加わってくるだろうと思っていましたね。

仙田　建物のまわりに円環状に駐車場や緑を配していく形になったし、外観も四方から形をつくっていったので、裏表があまりない感じです。

清水さんは東工大で私の研究室の出身でしたが、修士の研究で図書館を取り上げたんだよね。

清水　ちょうどデジタルによる変革が僕の学生時代に始まっていて、図書館建築がどのように変わっていくのかという視点を持っていたのですが、なかなか論文としてまとまらなくて（笑）。近い将来、図書館にどのような機能が必要になるのか、といったところをメインに考えていました。

仙田　今回の石川県立図書館のプロポーザルでは清水さんと一緒にいろいろなプランニングを行い、最終的に外側、外装の意匠を清水さんにまとめてもらったわけです。建物の高さ制限もあったわけで

Senda: This place is the former site of Kanazawa University's Faculty of Engineering. When we had a look around during the proposal phase, there were many cherry trees, as is often seen in school sites. The surrounding area is residential, so we decided to construct the building in the center of the premises.

We wanted to keep as much of the greenery as possible and arrange the parking space to surround the library. This inevitably led to placing entrances at various locations of the building. Mr. Yanagihara, what was your first impression of the site?

Yanagihara: The old school buildings had already been demolished when I first visited the site, but the road alignment of the campus was still there.

One of my initial thoughts was about the relationship with the neighboring shrine, Ueno Hachiman Shrine. This shrine has a thick layer of greenery that really caught my attention. The rest of the area is mostly residential, but I thought creating a link with this greenery would become the core of this project.

The car turnaround in front of the main building of Kanazawa University remained, where a few trees were left in the planting strip in the center of the turnaround. An impressive Japanese red pine tree called "Tagyousho" stood out particularly amongst them, which now stands in front of the library. This tree species is also planted throughout Kenrokuen, and my immediate reaction was to preserve this tree as it had been trained properly and had a good shape.

I also thought it would be better to keep the cherry trees. Existing trees already have good volume and presence incomparable to newly planted trees, so it was absolutely necessary to preserve them.

It was easy to envision this radial structure from the beginning of the project, where the library would sit in the center in relation to the large trees surrounding it. I was sure that this relationship would also extend to the shrine as well.

Senda: The parking space and greenery are arranged in a circle around the building. The façade was designed from all directions, so the concept of front and back of a building is almost nonexistent.

Mr. Shimizu, you are a graduate of my laboratory at Tokyo Institute of Technology. You researched libraries for your master's degree, didn't you?

Shimizu: The digital transformation had just started when I was a student, and I was interested in how library architecture would change. I struggled with writing the thesis though (laughs). My main focus was on what functions would be needed in libraries in the near future.

Senda: For this proposal for the Ishikawa Prefectural Library, Mr. Shimizu and I worked on various plans, and ultimately he finalized the design for the landscape and façade of the building. There were building height restrictions, but I think the way the elevation was created was quite special in the sense that the building would be approachable from

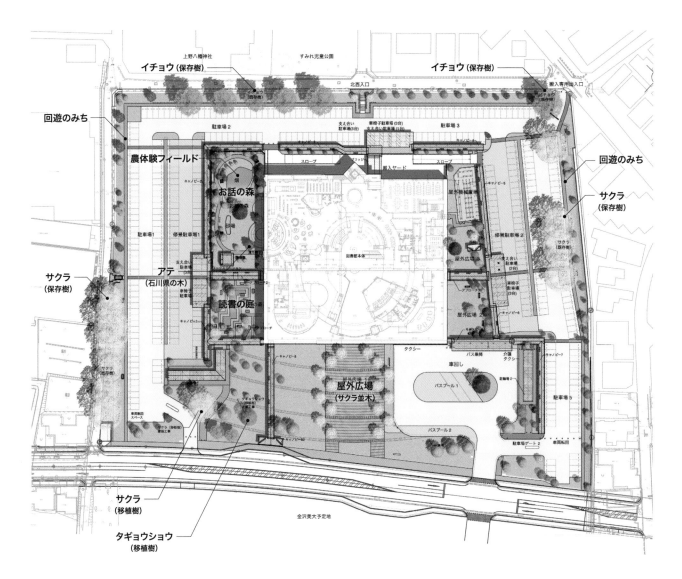

全体ランドスケープ平面図。サクラとイチョウの既存樹、サクラとタギョウショウの移植樹を取り込み、
建物南側正面に屋外広場、西側に「お話の森」「読書の庭」、東側に二つの芝生広場を配置（柳原）

すが、正面の道路はもちろん、どこからもアプローチしてくるという
意味で、立面のつくり方が結構特殊だったのではないか思うのですが。
清水　意匠はコンペの時から、だいぶ変わりましたね。ただ、昔から
僕が考えていたコンセプトに、割と繋がっている気がしているんです。
具体的には、どんどん街中から本屋がなくなっていく状況の中で、
図書館は自ら能動的に本を探すための施設というよりは、本を眺め
ながら歩いていくような、本屋のような公共施設に変わっていくの
ではないか、ということを考えていたんです。
その上で、今回は先生がおっしゃったように真ん中にドーンと建物
があるわけで、それは結構大きいなと思ったんです。それをヒュー
マンスケールに落とし込むようなやさしさを考えていたということ
がありますね。

all directions including the front road.

Shimizu: The design has changed a lot since the competition. But I feel
that it still connects to the concept I have had in mind for a while.
More specifically, while bookstores were disappearing from the city, I
was thinking that libraries would transform into public facilities like
bookstores, where people can look at books and wander around, rather
than a place where people actively search for a particular book.
And on top of that, as Mr. Senda mentioned, a massive building lies in
the middle of the site. That is quite impactful, and I was thinking about
how to gently bring it down to a human scale.

とても多様な石川県の植生
手を入れ、育てていくことが大事（柳原）

"威厳"と"親しみやすさ"を併せ持つ建築

An Architecture with Dignity and Approachability

仙田　そして、もう一つの大きなテーマが「工芸建築」だったわけですが。

清水　やはり、金沢に立つ建築である以上、地元の伝統や文化といったものを大事にしたいなと。最初は木虫籠のイメージから入っていきました。何より、県の方々とお会いするたびに、すごく自分たちの文化を大切にされているということを感じていました。

仙田　本を「めくる」というイメージ、ページとページの間みたいなものを大切にしていこうということと、工芸建築というところでタイルがポイントになりましたね。

清水　外壁の仕上げにはいろいろ候補を挙げましたよね。

仙田　乾式工法はあなたが提案してくれたのだけれど、結果的に非常によかったと思うね。

清水　やっぱり二層分でこの量のタイルなので、一番心配したのはエフロですよね。エフロが出てきたら目も当てられないので、まずはきれいに保ちやすいディテールというのが大事だったと思います。

仙田　国代（耐火工業所）さんには、エレベーションで結構な数の案をつくっていただきましたね。

清水　確かコンペの段階では、少し町家っぽくて、もうちょっと威厳が欲しいと言われた覚えがありますね（笑）

Senda: Another major concept was "*kogei* architecture" (architecture imbued with the spirit of authentic craftsmanship).

Shimizu: Considering we were designing architecture in the historic town of Kanazawa, it was important for us to embrace the local traditions and culture. This started with an image of the traditional wooden lattice windows, kimusuko. Above all, whenever I met with the locals, I felt that they really cherished their own culture.

Senda: We wanted to evoke the feeling of "flipping through the pages of a book", emulating the space between pages, and the tiles became a key feature of *kogei* architecture.

Shimizu: We explored various options for the exterior wall finish.

Senda: Opting for the dry construction method for tiles was your suggestion and it turned out really nicely.

Shimizu: I was concerned most about efflorescence because of the amount of tiles we were using for the two layers. Once it appears it becomes an eyesore, so it was important to focus on details that were easy to maintain its clean look.

Senda: The manufacturer, Kunishiro, proposed quite a few plans for the elevation.

Shimizu: I remember the client told us during the competition phase that they wanted more "dignity," since our proposal gave them an

仙田　「知の殿堂」だからね。

清水　でもクライアントからの要望が、よいきっかけになったと思いますね。"威厳"という言葉が気になって、スタディがあらぬ方に向かったりもしましたが（笑）、もう一度、本が主役であるという原点に立ち返ることになりました。

改めて本自体をテーマにして、ページをめくるということに着目し、最終的にそれぞれの外壁の端部を"めくる"形状にしたじゃないですか。それによって、ある程度の威厳をもたらすことができたのではないかと。柳原さんもポイントに挙げていた神社も威厳だけでなく、お祭りのように市民に開かれている部分もありますし、威厳と親しみやすさの両方をうまく取り入れられたかなと思います。

仙田　アプローチ的には、敷地に対して小立野の大通りから斜めに入っていくからね。そこにページが開いている感じを見せていくことは、割とうまくいったんじゃないかな。本当はもう少しカーブをつける予定だったんだけどね（笑）

清水　そうですね。図書館という施設の性格上、外光・西日対策などを考慮していくと、なかなか難しかったですね。

直射日光を避けるために、一つひとつのパネルの角度が細かく、全部決まっていますからね（苦笑）。現場で「この通りにしなくちゃいけないんですか」と聞かれて、この通りじゃないとダメなんですと。少しずつ、微妙に全部違うので、大変でした。

神社や日本建築の屋根の反りにも繋がると考えていて、当初は全部めくられている形状の案だったんですよね。さすがにクライアントから、全部はやめてくれと言われてしまったのですが、結果的にそうしなくてよかったですね。大変なことになっていたかもしれません。

impression of a traditional machiya townhouse (laughs).

Senda: It is the Hall of Knowledge after all.

Shimizu: But I think the client's request was a good turning point. I was intrigued by the word "dignity," and my research went off on a tangent sometimes (laughs), but we returned to the starting point that books were the protagonists of this project.

Focusing once again on books as the concept and the idea of flipping through book pages, we settled on an exterior wall structure where the edges were "flippable." This gave the building a certain degree of dignity. Just like how a shrine, which Mr. Yanagihara mentioned, carries a level of dignity but also shows a side that is welcoming to the public like festivals, I think we managed to create a good balance between dignity and approachability.

Senda: In terms of access, you enter the site diagonally from the main street in Kodatsuno. I think we succeeded in evoking a feeling of an open page once you enter the site. Even though the original plan was to add a little more curve (laughs).

Shimizu: That's right. Due to the nature of a library, it was challenging to consider measures against sunlight and afternoon light.

The angle of each panel had to be precisely calculated to avoid direct sunlight (laughs). The construction workers asked "Do they have to be this precise?" and I'd answer each time that they had to. Each panel angle is slightly different so it was incredibly hard work.

Initially, the plan was to create a structure where all the pages were turned so that it would link to the curved roofs of shrines and Japanese architecture. The client asked us not to flip the entire wall, which was the right decision. It could have been a nightmare.

Senda: We had to deal with the construction costs too. But we

威厳と親しみやすさの両方を表現することができた（清水）

仙田　工事費との兼ね合いもあったからね。でも最初からコンクリートパネルは、割とローコストでできそうだという話だったのですよ。

清水　スパンクリートという、コストパフォーマンスに優れた材料を使いました。製造元のスパンクリートコーポレーションに本気で検討していただけて、外壁の少しずつ角度をずらしながら、という作業に楽しんで取り組んでいただくことができたのではないかと思います。

were informed that the concrete panels could be done at a rather reasonable cost.

Shimizu: We used a material with an excellent cost-benefit performance called Spancrete. The manufacturer, Spancrete Corporation, gave us serious consideration, and I think they really enjoyed the process of shifting the angles of the façade one by one.

B-01
130×130 せっき質タイル
茶 斜十字凹+緑 斜十字凹：市松張り

外観デザイン検討CG。春分・夏至・秋分・冬至の現地における太陽光の角度を計算し、特に西日の直射日光を避けるように、外壁パネルそれぞれの角度と配置、端部の反りについて検討した。タイルの形状・色・配置については数多くのパターンを検討し、実物のタイルを近景・遠景から確認することで候補を絞り、現場にてモックアップを制作し、最終決定した（清水）

外壁タイルサンプル。斜め十字の凹型形状、外壁の反りに追従する最小のタイル寸法について、何度も試し焼きを行った。乾式工法として成立し、製品として担保できるタイルの大きさ・厚み・色合いを模索、検討した（清水）

図書館と共に成長していく緑
Greenery That Grows with the Library

仙田　工芸建築の外壁のリズムと外構の緑。今、正面のサクラが本当にきれいで華やかな感じですね。

柳原　実は最初に提案した樹種とは違うものなんです。いくつか異なる提案をしたのですが、最終的にクライアントの強い要望でソメイヨシノになりました。一番初めに花だけが咲いてほしいということで、その条件を突き詰めていくと、やっぱりソメイヨシノになるんですね。元々、周囲に植えられていたサクラがソメイヨシノでしたので、違う種類のサクラを提案していたのですが、花が一斉に咲く風景をつくりたいというリクエストでした。

今日、これだけ天気のいい日に一斉に咲いていて、花の白い色と背景の建物だけが視界に入ってくるという感じはすごくいいなと思いましたね。

仙田　サクラの老木もね。

柳原　すごくよかったです。最初はこれだけの老巨木を残すことに意味があるのか、というご意見もあったのですが、県の方からの後押しもあって、活用させていただくことになりました。

仙田　あのサクラの老木があることによって、ここがかつて金沢大学の工学部だったという土地の記憶が引き継がれていくからね。ここは図書館だから、そういう記録をしっかり残しておく必要があると思うのです。

あとは入口に連なっていくキャノピーも印象的だなと。いわゆる雪国ならではの植栽・外構計画になりました。

柳原　そうですね。今回いろいろ勉強させていただきましたが、石川県にはとても多様な植生があるということがよくわかりました。大きく言うと、能登半島、加賀地方、金沢では植生が異なり、海岸から高山帯までの標高によっても変わります。各地の里山等の人の営みの影響も加わって、実に多様性に富んでいます。でも、造園的に使える樹種は限られているんですね。その中からいくつか選び出して「おはなしの森」に植えることになりました。

仙田　この図書館は石川県内の各地域の様々な資源や文化を紹介する施設という位置づけなので、幼稚園や保育園のこどもたちのための園外保育で訪れていただくと、地元の植物や風土を身近に感じられるようになっているわけです。そういう場所を持っている図書館も、きわめて珍しいと思います。

柳原　「おはなしの森」の中に農園があって、リンゴとナシの木を植えているのですが、あれがどんどん育っていってほしいですね。おそらく農園のエリアは、毎年のように何かしら手が加えられると思うので、年を重ねるごとにどんどん風景が変わっていくと思いますし、現状でもその下地がよくでき上がっていると思います。

仙田　造園というものは建築と違って、5年後、10年後と、どんどん変化して成長しますね。

Senda: The rhythm of the *kogei* architecture façade and green landscape. The cherry blossoms in the front are really beautiful and stunning right now.

Yanagihara: They are actually a different species from the initial proposal. We suggested a few options but ultimately decided on "somei-yoshino" as per the client's strong request. They wanted only flowers to bloom first, and only "somei-yoshino" fits this requirement. The existing cherry trees were already "somei-yoshino", so we proposed different species for variety, but the client wanted to create a landscape where all the flowers bloom at once.

On a beautiful day like today, it's wonderful to see them all in flower—a view of only the whites of the flowers and the building as a backdrop.

Senda: Not to mention the old cherry trees.

Yanagihara: It was fantastic. There were mixed opinions at first about whether it would be worth saving such an ancient tree, but with encouragement from the prefectural government, we decided to make the most of it.

Senda: That old cherry tree carries the memory of the land that was once the Faculty of Engineering at Kanazawa University. Since this is a library, I think it is especially important that we keep such a record.

The tree canopies that continue to the entrance are also remarkable. The planting and landscape design became something unique to snowy regions.

Yanagihara: True. I learned a lot on this project, especially that Ishikawa has a surprisingly diverse vegetation.

Broadly speaking, the vegetation differs between the Noto Peninsula, Kaga region, and Kanazawa, and it varies depending on elevation from coast to alpine. Then there are the satoyamas in each region where there is influence of human activities, it is truly diverse. But tree choice for landscaping is limited. We selected a few of them and designed to plant them as "Ohanashi no mori (Narrative Forest)."

Senda: This library serves as a cultural and educational hub that introduces various materials and cultures in each region in Ishikawa Prefecture. When children from kindergartens and nursery schools visit the library on their field trips, they can become familiar with local plants and the climate. I think it is very rare for a library to hold such characters.

Yanagihara: There is a farm in "Ohanashi no mori" where we have planted apples and pears. I hope they will continue to grow. The farm area will probably have someone tending to it every year, so the landscape will change as the years go by, and I think the current groundwork is well prepared for it.

Senda: Unlike architecture, landscape continues to change and grow in the following 5, 10 years, and so on.

Yanagihara: When a facility is freshly completed, there is still a distant feel to the place. As time passes, it will settle down and blend in with

柳原　施設ができ上がったばかりの頃はまだまだ、よそよそしい感じがありますからね。これから時間を経るごとに落ち着いて、なじんでくるということだと思います。

仙田　いわゆる環境としてのポテンシャルという意味では、樹木の成長などによって大きく付加価値が向上していくのではないかな。建築自体も時間が経って、味が出てくるとか、親しみやすさみたいなものを発揮していくと思う。

柳原　建築も植物もメンテナンスが大事ですよね。人工的な庭や農園というものは、人が手を入れることが基本になりますから。そこは図書館と共に、年を重ねていくにつれて、よくなっていくものと思います。

the surroundings.

Senda: In terms of the potential of the environment, I think the trees maturing and other factors will add great value to the place. The architecture itself will mature over time and develop its own character and display a sense of familiarity.

Yanagihara: Maintenance is important in both architecture and plants. Anything manmade, like a garden or farm, basically needs human intervention. It will improve as it ages alongside the library.

タイルで施設のキャラクターを表現する

Portraying Character through Tiles

仙田　我々はエントランスの真ん中にちょっとした広場もつくったんですよね。将来的にあそこをマルシェにして、フードカーも入れられるようにしてあります。

柳原　図書館の中と外を立体的に、うまく使っていけたらいいですね。

仙田　その広場の正面には金沢美術工芸大学がこの秋にオープンするんですよね。それも結構大きな要素です。

柳原　また、人の流れが変わってきて、図書館の方にも学生たちがあふれ出てくるんじゃないかと（笑）

仙田　我々は図書館の外壁のタイルを市松模様にしたわけですが、大学の外観、外構との相乗効果も楽しみです。

清水　最終的に茶色と緑の市松になったわけですが、かなり色味を検討しましたね。

仙田　それから、タイルに影をどのように付けられるかにもこだわりました。

清水　影という意味では、予想していなかった効果が出たのが面白かったですね。今回はタイルの一つひとつに、斜めに十字の模様を入れているのですが、遠目から見ると、真四角のタイルの角が丸く見えるんですよ。あれは全く予期していませんでした。

先生と現場に来た時に「あれ、タイルなんか丸くないか、まずいな」と思ったんですけど、目の錯覚なんですよね。かわいらしくて、すごくいい効果だなと。そういうこともあってか、建物も思っているよりも低く見えて、すごく親しみやすくなったなと思いました。

仙田　十字模様のタイルは変形しないギリギリのところを狙って、ずいぶん試作品をつくりましたね。

清水　県の方とも実際に並べてみて、離れるとどう見えるかという

Senda: We also created a spacious square by the entrance foyer. It can be used to hold farmer's markets in the future with enough room for food trucks.

Yanagihara: It would be nice to see both the inside and outside of the library being used in depth.

Senda: Across this square, the Kanazawa College of Art will open this autumn. This is also another impacting factor.

Yanagihara: The flow of people will change again, and the library will overflow with students (laughs).

Senda: We decided on a checkerboard pattern for the tiles on the library façade, and I'm looking forward to seeing how it will play off against the university's landscape and exterior, collectively complementing each other.

Shimizu: We settled on a brown and green checkerboard pattern, but we contemplated quite a bit on color.

Senda: We were also meticulous about how to create shadows on the tiles.

Shimizu: In terms of shadows, we were pleasantly surprised by their effects. Each of the tiles has a diagonal cross-groove pattern, which from a distance, makes the sharp corners of the tile look rounded. It was completely unexpected.

When Mr. Senda and I arrived on site, I thought, "Oh no, the tiles look rounded …", but it was actually an optical illusion. It's charming and actually a very nice effect. Perhaps because of this optical effect, the building looks lower than expected and is much more approachable.

Senda: We searched for the very limit where the tiles would not deform and made a lot of prototypes of the cross-shaped tiles.

Shimizu: We actually placed the tiles with staff of the prefectural

のをチェックしました。近くよりは遠目の方が魅力的な表情になるので、それがすごくよかったなと思いますね。

仙田　二つの色を使って、また、それぞれにまたムラがあるから面白いよね。

そういう風に我々の思い入れを反映させたことで、図書館の外壁の機能がどういうものか、考えるきっかけになったと思うのですが。

清水　そうですね。今回、僕はあまり図書館という捉え方をしていなかったかもしれません。同じ図書館というビルディングタイプでも、異なる考え方で取り組むと、新たなキャラクターや役割が生まれてくるという、よい事例になったのではないかと思います。

government and checked how they would look from a distance. They look more attractive from a distance than up close, so it was a great idea.

Senda: On top of the duotone effect, it's interesting to see the variations in the color of each tile.

I think that reflecting our sentiments into the design gave us a chance to think about the functions of a library exterior wall.

Shimizu: I agree. With this project, I wasn't looking at it as a library project per se. This is a great example of how a different perspective on the same building type as a library can inspire the creation of new characteristics and functions.

屋内と屋外が循環し、まちに広がっていく図書館

A library That Seamlessly Blends the Indoors and Outdoors, Extending throughout the City

仙田　私がこの図書館のプロポーザルに取り組む時のモチーフになったのが、友人の造園家の話です。東京都の公園緑地部長を務めて、井の頭公園を設計された方ですね。彼に取材した「井の頭公園100年」という新聞記事の中で、ご家族に先立たれた老境の友人は毎日井の頭公園を散策して、こどもたちが遊んでいるのを眺めながら、元気に生きることができていると述べておられるんです。

そんな、生きる力をもたらす、歩き回れる公園のような図書館。「ワンダリング」をテーマにして、中も外も遊環構造にして回遊できる施設がつくれないかと考えたわけです。

柳原　図書館という施設は一般的には、本を読む場所という風に用途が特定されるのですが、公園という場の機能は一つではないんですよね。人それぞれの目的を持って、フラッと訪れて、なんとなくそこにいるというようなことを許容してくれる。おそらく、ここはそういう図書館になるんだろうなと、僕なりには理解していました。ただ僕は先生が公園や庭園のように回遊をするということをおっしゃっているのを聞いていて、それは比喩なのだろうと思っていたんです。ところが、実際にでき上がってきた時に、比喩ではなくて、そのような建築になっているというのがわかって、本当にそういうことが可能なのだと驚いた次第です。まさに建物に包容力があって、いろいろな人を受け入れるような場になっているのだなと。

仙田　そうですね。技術的な部分で言うと、BDS（Book Detection System、主に図書館におけるセキュリティシステム）という入館装置がありますよね、あれは本の管理のために使われているのだけれど、うまく機能させて、館外に本をどんどん持ち出していけるようになるとさらにいいと思うんです（笑）。外構や地域全体をBDSで管理するぐらいになればいいと考えているのですが、現状でそのように

Senda: When I started working on the proposal for this library, I was inspired by the story of my friend landscape designer. He was the head of the Tokyo Metropolitan Government Bureau of Construction and designed Inokashira Park. In a newspaper article titled "100 Years of Inokashira Park," my friend, in his old age, says he was preceded in death by his family, and he strolls around Inokashira Park every day and watches children playing, which gives him the energy to live well.

Then I thought of a library that permeates vitality and is also a park to wander around. With "wandering" as a concept, we wanted to create a facility with a circular play system that seamlessly integrates the in with the out, where people can walk around.

Yanagihara: Generally, a library is a place to read books, but a park has more than one function. Each with its own purpose, people can wander in and meander. It allows you to just exist in the space. My understanding was that this library was going to become such a place. But I thought Mr. Senda was speaking metaphorically when he spoke about wandering in the library like a park or garden.

Yet, when the building was completed, I realized that it had transformed into actual architecture, not just a metaphor, and I was genuinely amazed that it was indeed possible. The building is truly accommodating and accepting of all types of people.

Senda: I think so. When looking at the technology aspect, there is a security system normally used in libraries called BDS (Book Detection System). This is used for book management, but if it were to work effectively, I think it would be even better if people could take out books freely from the building (laughs). Wouldn't it be great if we could manage the landscape, or better yet, the entire region with BDS? However, currently it only extends up to the "Children's Area."

Yanagihara: I would say the "Children's Area" alone is quite groundbreaking.

なっているのは「こどもエリア」だけなんですよね。

柳原　「こどもエリア」だけでも、相当画期的だと思いますよ。

仙田　そういう意味では次の段階では、もう少し外部の広いエリアまで含めた、図書館のつくり込みができるといいよね。移動図書館的なモバイルブックカーとか、屋外に屋根付きの書架があるとかさ。屋内と屋外が連関していくといいよね。

以前、私は中国の園林を見て、すごく感心したんだよね。特に蘇州の古典園林。留園とか獅子林など、たくさんあるのですが、日本の庭園と比べると圧倒的に集客力があるんだよね。

柳原　観光地的ということですか？

仙田　圧倒的に座るところが多いんです。

柳原　確かに、回廊のところに長椅子が連続していますね。

仙田　あの椅子の形態が長く居続けるということを可能にしていると思うんだよね。

柳原　日本では大抵、ベンチの数や大きさが限られていますよね。

仙田　この図書館でも、本棚のすぐそばに、座るところがずらっとあるでしょう。それは屋外でも可能なのではないかと思うんですよ。

柳原　そもそも中国の庭園は中と外が、本当に繋がっている感じがありますね。普通に歩いていると中を通って、外に出て、また中に入ってみたいな動線ができていますね。

仙田　中国の園林には基本的には廊があるから、傘をささないで、全部中から見られるようになっているからね。だから、ここでも、できれば建物のまわりをめぐるエリアをつくって、BDSでコントロールするとかね。そういうことを夢見ているのですが。

清水　駐車場の外周にも、樹木が植わっているのにつれて、舗装さ

Senda: In that sense, it would be great if the next design phase of this project could include a wider area surrounding the library. A mobile public library like a book truck, or outdoor bookshelves with a roof. It would be nice to see even more connection between the indoor and outdoor areas.

I was really impressed by the traditional Chinese gardens which I visited in the past. Especially the classical gardens of Suzhou. There's a variety of gardens like the Lingering Garden and the Lion Grove Garden. When compared to Japanese gardens, they are exceptionally effective at attracting visitors.

Yanagihara: Do you mean as a tourist spot?

Senda: The number of seating areas they have is incredible.

Yanagihara: True. They have a series of benches in the corridor.

Senda: I think the form of those seats allows people to stay there for a long time.

Yanagihara: In Japan, the number and size of benches are usually limited.

Senda: In this library, you see many seats arranged near bookshelves. I think we can do the same outdoors too.

Yanagihara: In the first place, the classical Chinese gardens have a sense of integration between the indoors and outdoors. The paths naturally lead you to walk inside and out, and back inside again.

Senda: Traditional Chinese gardens basically have corridors, so you are able to view everything from inside without an umbrella. My dream is to create a similar effect at the library, like an area that circulates around the building, controlled by BDS.

Shimizu: There are trees planted around the perimeter of the parking area. And a paved road along it. I had a walk around there and would

あのサクラの老木によって土地の記憶が引き継がれていく（仙田）

れた道がありますよね。あそこを歩いてみたのですが、確かにそういう仕組みが欲しいですね（笑）

仙田　そうそう、あの外周に本があるといいよね。現状で、外構までも含めたかたちで図書館を整えることができたから、それを拡大していくということを次の段階として考えていければいいですね。

——そのような遊環構造の発展・進化と、外観の「めくる」形状とは、どのような関係にあるのでしょうか。

仙田　建物にポーラス（porous）、"穴"が開いているのがポイントだと考えているんです。建物が閉じられているのではなくて、（建物をめくって）開かれて、"穴"が開くことによって、中と外が繋がって、循環し、別の意味を持つようになるということかな。

清水　四角い敷地の真ん中に丸いドームが入っているので、それが視覚的にも放射状に外に抜けていくという意味で、内部の回遊動線が外構に繋がっていくといいなという思いがありましたね。

——入れ子構造にもなっているわけですね。

柳原　入れ子構造というのはある意味で、遊環構造と同じなのですが、始まりのあとに終わりがあるのではなく、始まりと終わりがごっちゃになっていて、それこそ始まりも終わりもないという感じですね。
一般的には、外部に都市的な世界があって、そこから建物の内部にたどり着くまでの中間に外構があるのですが、この図書館では館内にも日常的な外の世界が広がっている。また、常に循環していて、館外に出ても中にいるような感覚が生まれているのかなと。
だから、先ほど仙田先生がおっしゃったように、図書館をさらに外に広げていくという意味で、本を館外に持ち出せるようになったら、面白いですよね。中と外が融合して、図書館が都市の中に染み出すようになっていく。そういうイメージでこの図書館が成長していったらいいですね。

仙田　イベントという意味でもね。今、屋内広場でピアノの演奏会など、様々な催しが行われているでしょう。これから、もう少しセキュリティエリアを広げられれば、屋外でも開催できるし、企画のバリエーションも増やしていけるよね。田村館長にも提案してみよう。

2023年3月28日収録

---

certainly like to see such a system in place (laughs).

Senda: Yes, it would be nice to have a book in hand at that perimeter, right? We were able to arrange the library in a way that includes that landscape, and it would be ideal if we could continue to think about expanding it as the next step.

——How does the development and evolution of such a circular structure relate to the "turning the pages" shape of the façade?

Senda: I think the key point is that the building is porous. The building isn't confined and opens up through "flipping the pages" of the building. By opening the "pores," it connects the inside with the outside, circulates, and takes on a different meaning.

Shimizu: The round dome lies right in the middle of a square site. It visually radiates outwards. I wanted the interior circulation lines in the library to extend into the landscape.

——So it is a nested structure.

Yanagihara: In a sense, a nested structure is the same thing as a circular play system. The beginning isn't necessarily followed by an end, but all are mixed up, so there really isn't a beginning or an end.

Generally speaking, on the outside lies an urban world, and the landscape exists in the space between outside and inside before arriving inside a building. But with this library, the daily outside world expands inside the building. It is constantly circulating and creates a sense of being inside, even when you are outside the building.

Therefore, as Mr. Senda mentioned earlier, it would be fascinating if books could be taken out of the library to further expand the library outside. Blending the inside with the outside, the library will seep into the city. I hope the library grows with this vision.

Senda: The same can be said about events, too. Currently, various programs take place in the indoor foyer, such as piano concerts. If we can expand the security area, we can hold events outdoors as well and increase the variety of the programs. Let's propose this to the library director, Mr. Tamura.

Interviewed on March 28, 2023

すでにある物語を大切にするのが環境デザイン。金沢大学工学部の置き土産として残されたタギョウショウを見上げる。

サクラ咲く季節は美しい屋外広場。屋内広場と一体となって、様々な文化的・商業的な催しの展開が期待される。図書館正面の外観は工芸建築として正面性を強調し、外壁コンクリートパネルが平面的に雁行している。

来訪者を雨や日差しから守ってくれるキャノピー（ひさし）。
外壁と共に、凛とした佇まいの建築を演出する重要な要素となっている。

（左）金沢大学工学部時代からのサクラの老木を活かしている。

（上）こどもエリアの屋外はおはなしの森と農体験フィールドにより構成されている。県内のこども園や保育園、幼稚園、
　　　小学校低学年の園外保育・校外授業とも十分に連携することが期待される。

（下）おはなしの森のおはなし広場。室内の小さなブックコロシアムと対峙している。

文化交流エリアの屋内広場から、屋外広場と金沢美術工芸大学の校舎を
見る。図書館と連携した様々な授業やアートシーンが展開されるだろう。

金沢美術工芸大学（撮影時建設中）を望む。図書館は壁が多いという原則
を活かしつつ、建築はポーラス（多孔質）でなければならない。タイルが
貼られた外壁コンクリートパネルの隙間は、図書館にいる人にとっては
安心基地であり、眺望の場でもある。

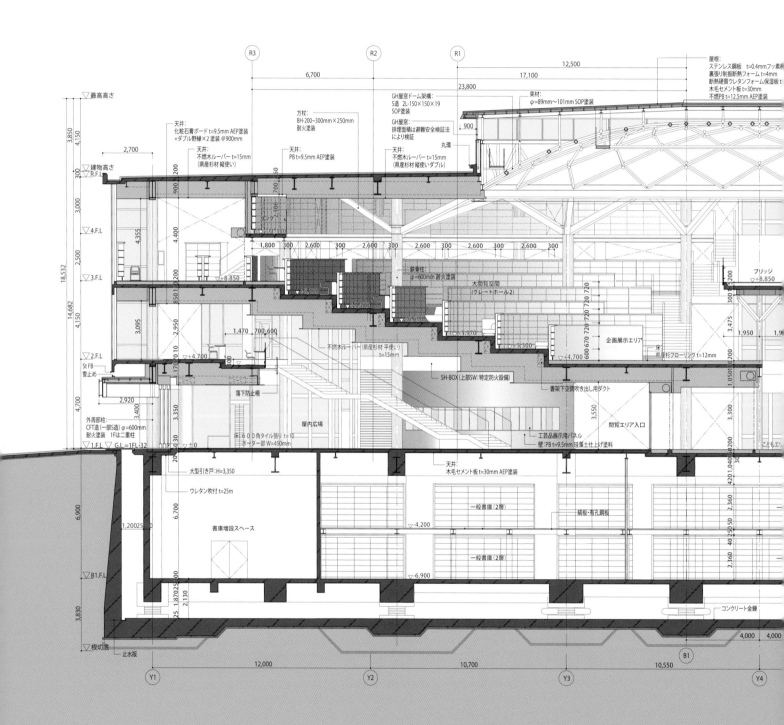

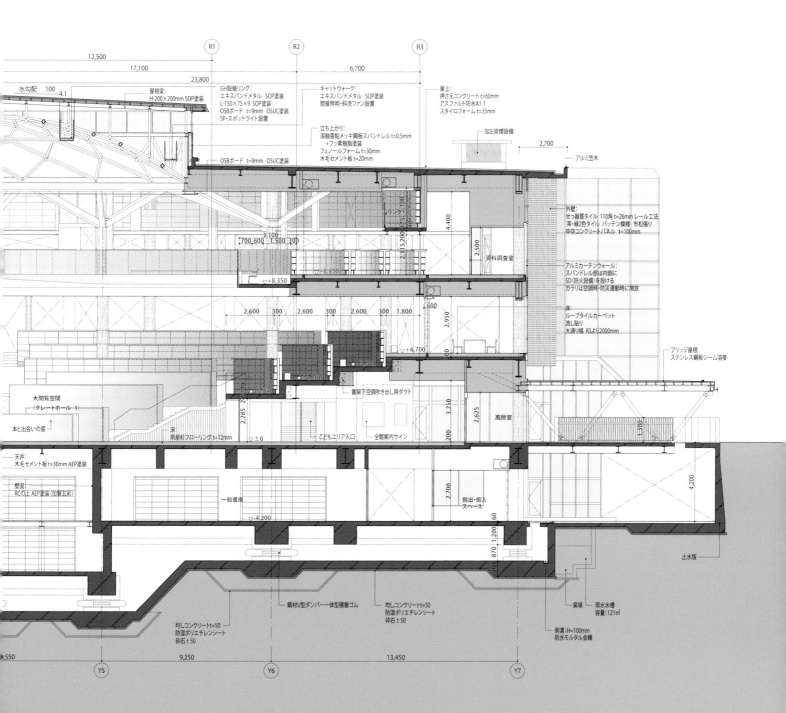

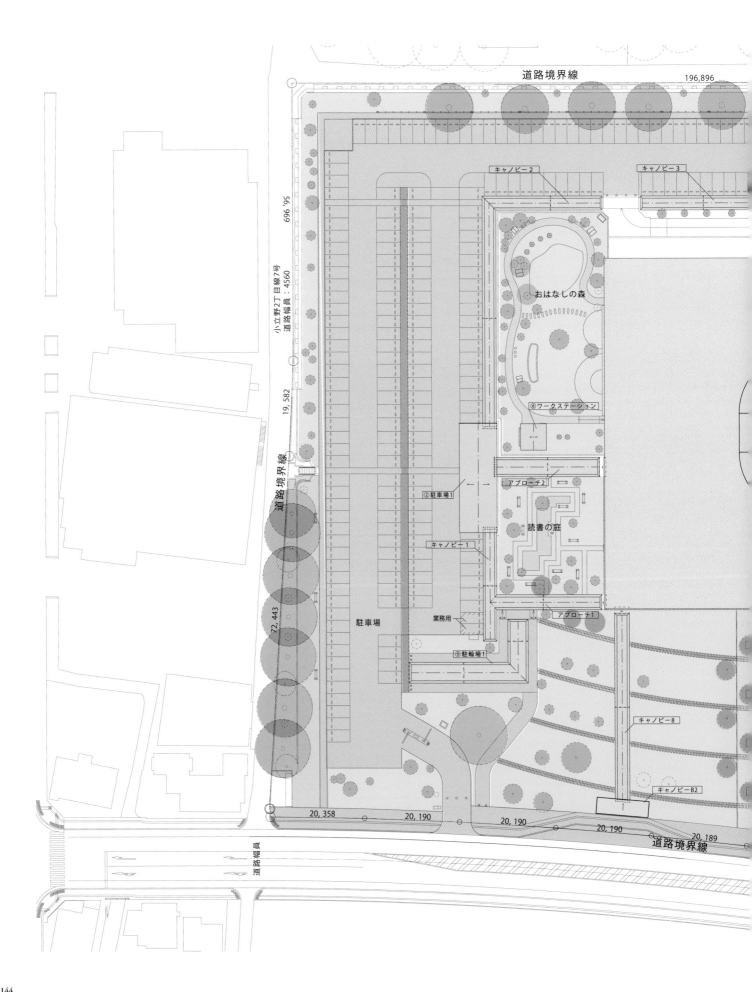

道路境界線　　　　　　　　　　　196,896

696 '95

小立野2丁目線7号
道路幅員：4560

19,582

道路境界線

72,443

キャノピー2　　　　　　　　　　キャノピー3

おはなしの森

⑧ワークステーション

②駐車場1　　　アプローチ2

読書の庭

キャノピー1

駐車場　　　　業務用　　　　アプローチ1

⑤駐輪場1

キャノピー8

キャノピーB2

20,358　　　　20,190　　　　20,190　　　　20,190　　　　20,189

道路境界線

道路幅員

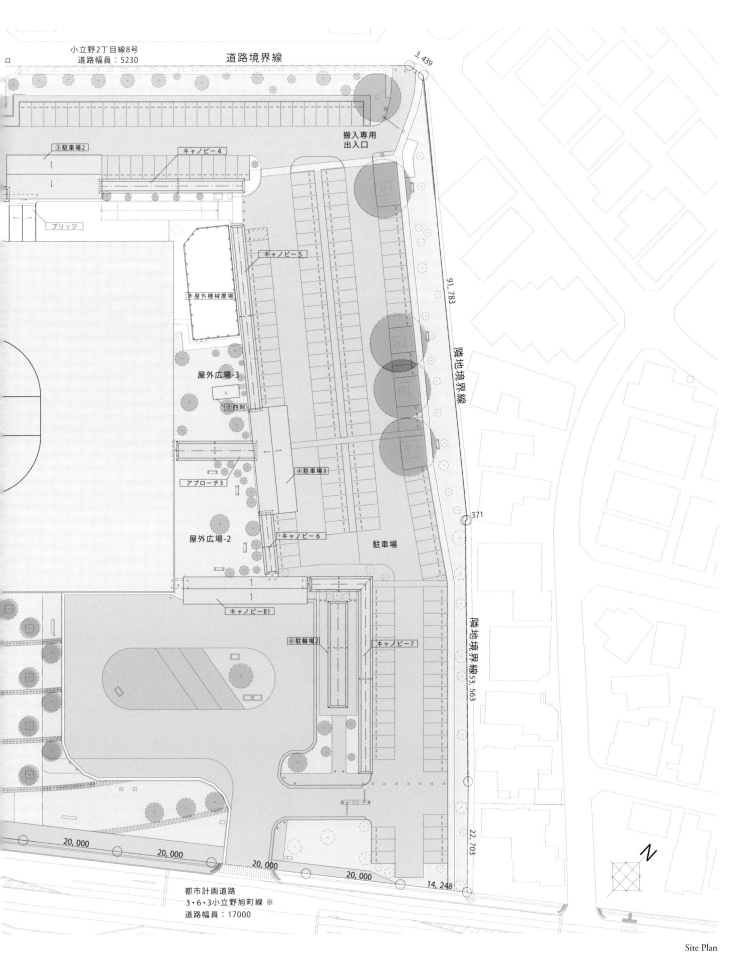

小立野2丁目線8号
道路幅員：5230

道路境界線

3,439

搬入専用
出入口

③駐車場2

キャノピー4

ブリッジ

キャノピー5

※屋外機械置場

屋外広場-3

⑦四阿

④駐車場3

アプローチ3

屋外広場-2

キャノピー6

駐車場

91,783

隣地境界線

371

キャノピーB1

⑥駐輪場2

キャノピー7

隣地境界線 53,563

22,703

20,000

20,000

20,000

20,000

14,248

都市計画道路
3・6・3小立野旭町線 ※
道路幅員：17000

Site Plan

145

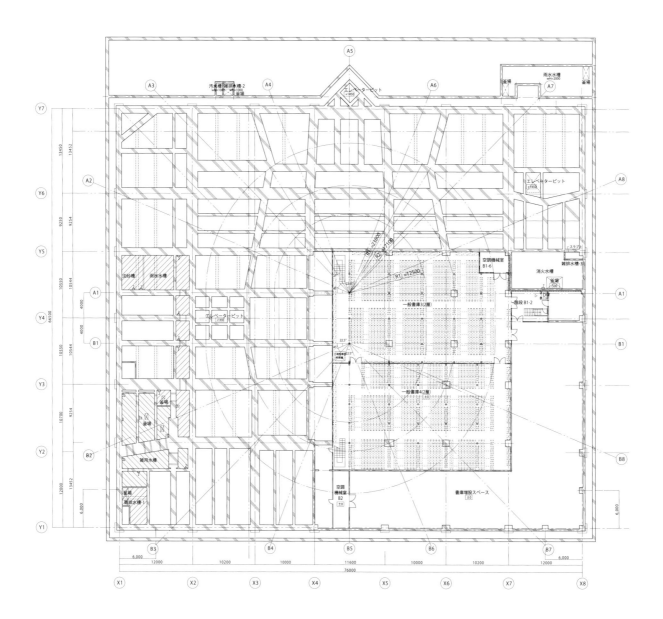

Pit Floor Plan

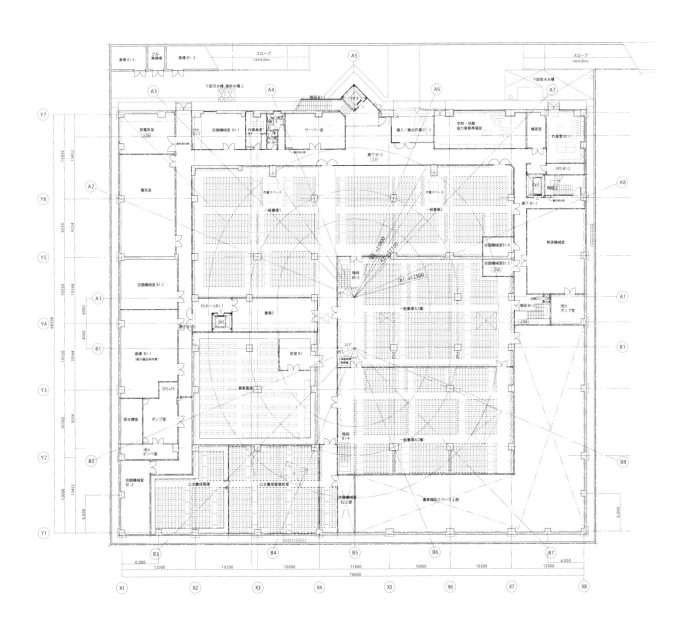

Basement Floor Plan

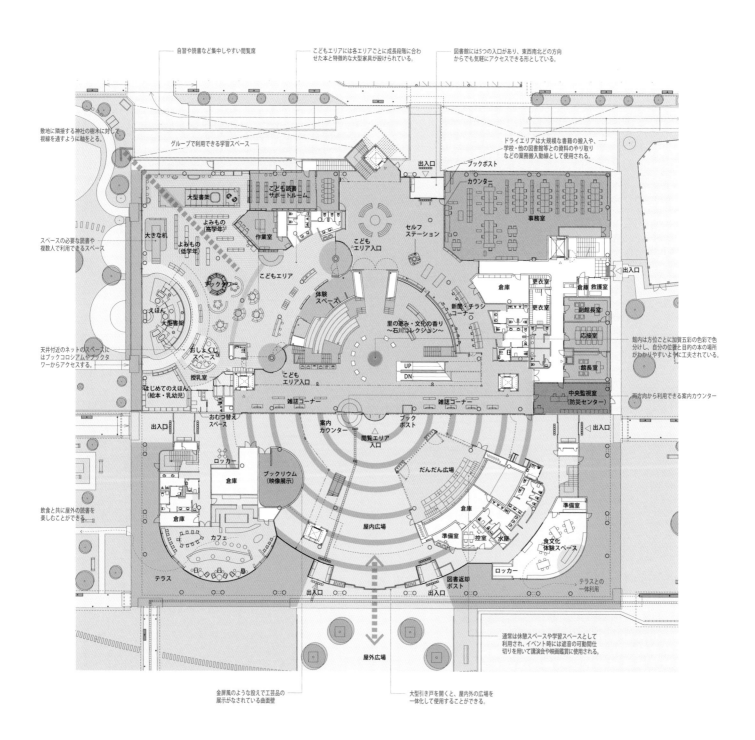

自習や読書など集中しやすい閲覧席

こどもエリアには各エリアごとに成長段階に合わせた本と特徴的な大型家具が設けられている。

図書館には5つの入口があり、東西南北どの方向からでも気軽にアクセスできる形としている。

敷地に隣接する神社の樹木に対して視線を通すように軸をとる。

グループで利用できる学習スペース

出入口

ブックポスト

ドライエリアは大規模な書籍の搬入や、学校・他の図書館等との資料のやり取りなどの業務搬入動線として使用される。

カウンター

大型書架

こども読書サポートルーム

事務室

よみもの（高学年）

大きな机

こどもエリア入口

セルフステーション

よみもの（低学年）

作業室

スペースの必要な読書や複数人で利用できるスペース

こどもエリア

体験スペース

新聞・チラシコーナー

倉庫

更衣室

倉庫 救護室

ブックタワー

えほん

大型書架

里の恵み・文化の香り〜石川コレクション〜

更衣室

副館長室

応接室

天井付近のネットのスペースにはブックコロシアムやブックタワーからアクセスする。

おしょくしスペース

授乳室

こどもエリア入口

UP
DN

館長室

はじめてのえほん（絵本・乳幼児）

館内は方位ごとに加賀五彩の色彩で色分けし、自分の位置と目的の本の場所がわかりやすいように工夫されている。

中央監視室（防災センター）

両方向から利用できる案内カウンター

雑誌コーナー

雑誌コーナー

おむつ替えスペース

出入口

案内カウンター

ブックポスト

閲覧エリア入口

出入口

ロッカー

倉庫

ブックリウム（映像展示）

だんだん広場

倉庫

準備室

飲食と共に屋外の読書を楽しむことができる

倉庫

屋内広場

準備室

控室

水屋

食文化体験スペース

カフェ

ロッカー

テラス

図書返却ポスト

テラスとの一体利用

出入口

出入口

屋外広場

通常は休憩スペースや学習スペースとして利用され、イベント時には遮音の可動間仕切りを用いて講演会や映画鑑賞に使用される。

金屏風のような設えで工芸品の展示がなされている曲面壁

大型引き戸を開くと、屋内外の広場を一体化して使用することができる。

1st Floor Plan and Color Scheme

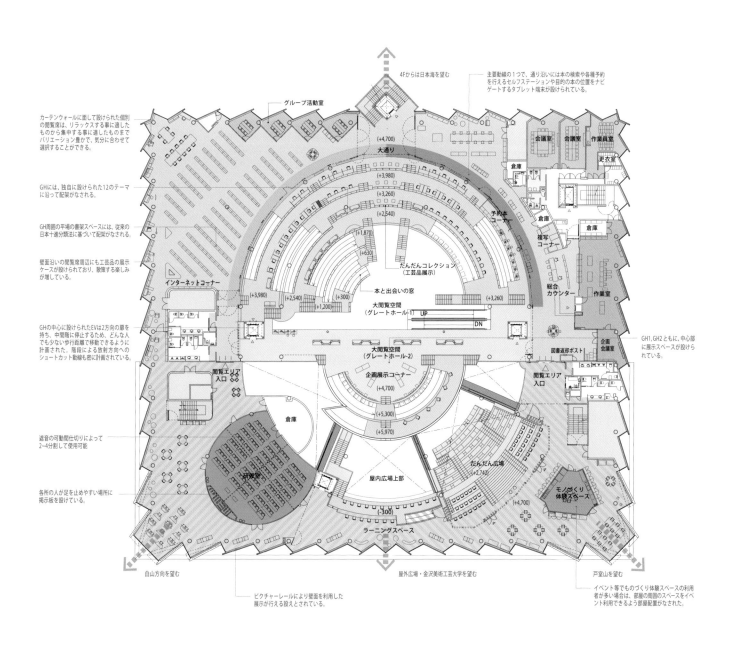

カーテンウォールに面して設けられた個別
の閲覧席は、リラックスする事に適した
ものから集中する事に適したものまで
バリエーション豊かで、気分に合わせて
選択することができる。

GHには、独自に設けられた12のテーマ
に沿って配架がなされる。

GH周囲の平場の書架スペースには、従来の
日本十進分類法に基づいて配架がなされる。

壁面沿いの閲覧席周辺にも工芸品の展示
ケースが設けられており、散策する楽しみ
が増している。

GHの中心に設けられたEVは2方向の扉を
持ち、中間階に停止するため、どんな人
でも少ない歩行距離で移動できるように
計画された。階段による放射方向への
ショートカット動線も密に計画されている。

遮音の可動間仕切りによって
2〜4分割して使用可能

各所の人が足を止めやすい場所に
掲示板を設けている。

グループ活動室

4Fからは日本海を望む

主要動線の1つで、通り沿いには本の検索や各種予約
を行えるセルフステーションや目的の本の位置をナビ
ゲートするタブレット端末が設けられている。

会議室　会議室　作業員室
更衣室
倉庫

大通り
(+4,700)
(+3,980)
(+3,260)
(+2,540)
(+1,870)
(+630)

予約本
コーナー
倉庫
複写
コーナー

総合
カウンター
作業室

だんだんコレクション
(工芸品展示)

インターネットコーナー
(+3,980) (+2,540) (+300)
(+1,200)
本と出会いの窓

(+3,260)

大閲覧空間
(グレートホール-1)　UP
DN

図書返却ポスト

閲覧エリア
入口

企画
会議室

GH1、GH2ともに、中心部
に展示スペースが設けら
れている。

大閲覧空間
(グレートホール-2)

倉庫

企画展示コーナー
(+4,700)
(+5,300)
(+5,970)

閲覧エリア
入口

研修室

屋内広場上部

だんだん広場
(+2,742)

モノづくり
体験スペース

(-300)

(+4,700)

ラーニングスペース

白山方向を望む

屋外広場・金沢美術工芸大学を望む

戸室山を望む

ピクチャーレールにより壁面を利用した
展示が行える設えとされている。

イベント等でのものづくり体験スペースの利用
者が多い場合は、部屋の周囲のスペースをイベ
ント利用できるよう部屋配置がなされた。

2nd Floor Plan and Color Scheme

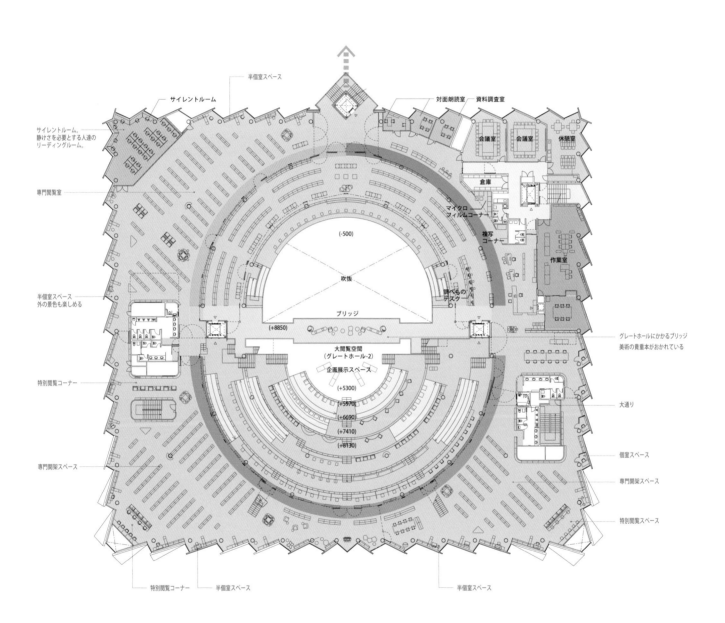

サイレントルーム

半個室スペース

対面朗読室 資料調査室

サイレントルーム。
静けさを必要とする人達の
リーディングルーム。

会議室 会議室 休憩室

専門閲覧室

倉庫

マイクロ
フィルムコーナー

複写
コーナー

作業室

(-500)

吹抜

ブリッジ

調べもの
デスク

半個室スペース
外の景色も楽しめる

(+8850)

大閲覧空間
(グレートホール-2)

グレートホールにかかるブリッジ
美術の貴重本がおかれている

企画展示スペース

特別閲覧コーナー

(+5300)

(+5970)

(+6690)

大通り

(+7410)

個室スペース

(+8130)

専門開架スペース

専門開架スペース

特別閲覧スペース

特別閲覧コーナー 半個室スペース

半個室スペース

3rd Floor Plan and Color Scheme

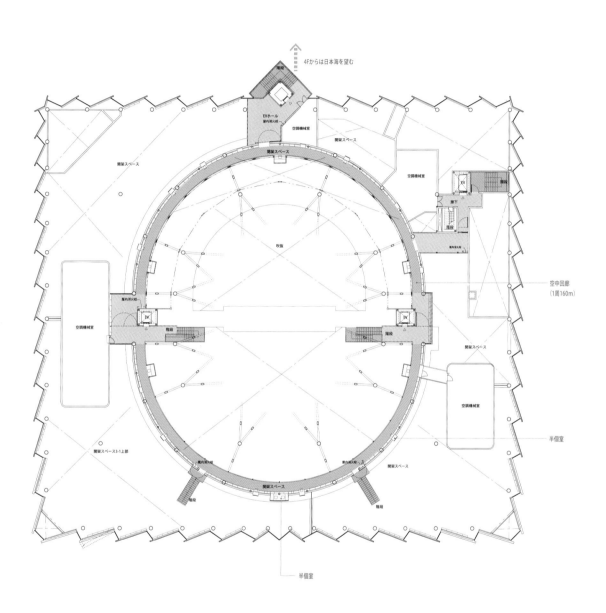

4F からは日本海を望む

階段

EVホール
屋内消火栓

空調機械室

開架スペース

開架スペース

開架スペース

空調機械室

EV

書庫

廊下

階段

吹抜

空中回廊
(1周160m)

屋内消火栓

空調機械室

階段

EV

階段

半個室

開架スペース3-1上部

屋内消火栓

屋内消火栓

開架スペース

階段

開架スペース

階段

半個室

4th Floor Plan

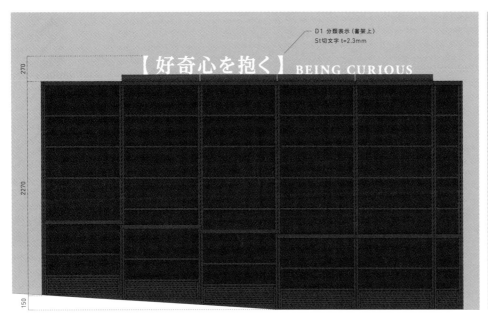

D1 分類表示（書架上）
St切文字 t=2.3mm

【好奇心を抱く】 BEING CURIOUS

270

2270

150

455

85

2545 200

D2 書架No.
シート切文字

D3 分類表示（側板）
プレート脱着式
出力シート貼包み

20 75

200

285

s 01

1650

Bookshelf Elevation

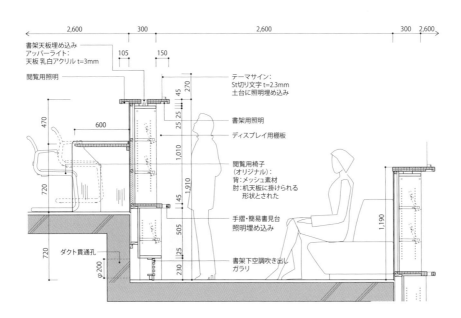

2,600　　300　　　　2,600　　　　300　2,600

書架天板埋め込み
アッパーライト：
天板 乳白アクリル t=3mm

閲覧用照明

105　　150

470

600

720

720

φ 200

ダクト貫通孔

45 270
25 25
1,010
1,910
45
505
125
230

テーマサイン：
St切り文字 t=2.3mm
土台に照明埋め込み

書架用照明
ディスプレイ用棚板

閲覧用椅子
（オリジナル）：
背：メッシュ素材
肘：机天板に掛けられる
　　形状とされた

手摺・簡易書見台
照明埋め込み

書架下空調吹き出し
ガラリ

1,190

GH Section Detail

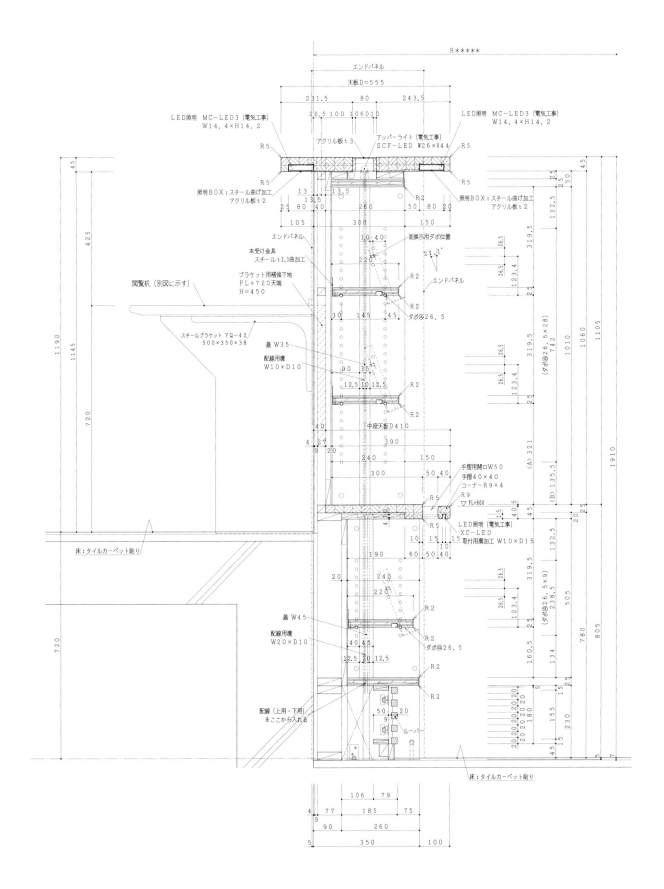

LED照明 MC-LED3（電気工事）
W14.4×H14.2

LED照明 MC-LED3（電気工事）
W14.4×H14.2

R5
アクリル板 t 3
アッパーライト（電気工事）
SCF-LED W26×H44
R5

R5
R5

照明BOX：スチール曲げ加工
アクリル板 t 2

照明BOX：スチール曲げ加工
アクリル板 t 2

エンドパネル

エンドパネル
天板D=555

エンドパネル

本受け金具
スチールt 2.3曲げ加工

面展示用ダボ位置

ブラケット用補強下地
FL+720天端
H=450

エンドパネル

閲覧机（別図に示す）

ダボ@26.5

スチールブラケット YQ-42
500×350×38

蓋 W35

配線用溝
W10×D10

中段天板D410

手摺用開口W50
手摺40×40
コーナーR9×4
R9
▽FL+800

LED照明（電気工事）
XC-LED
取付用溝加工 W10×D15

床：タイルカーペット貼り

蓋 W45

配線用溝
W20×D10

ダボ@26.5

配線（上用・下用）
をここから入れる

ルーバー

床：タイルカーペット貼り

Bookshelf Detail Section

153

石川県立図書館 建築概要

Architectural Overview

所在地　　石川県金沢市小立野2丁目43番1号
主要用途　図書館・集会場
建主　　　石川県
総括　　　仙田満
　　　　　石川県土木部営繕課

設計・監理 ───────────────────

建築　環境デザイン研究所
　　　担当／仙田満　野村朋広　久住郁子　町田潤哉
　　　　　　田中秋水　陳詩微　林恒視（元所員）

　　　石川県土木部営繕課
　　　担当／矢尾志津江　中橋英志　嘉門佳顕
　　　　　　木村和哉　中谷内裕徳　清坐早苗

監理協力　村井祐二

構造　金箱構造設計事務所
　　　担当／金箱温春　望月泰宏

設備　建築設備設計研究所
　　　担当／増田祥久　須賀栄治

家具・什器　設計・監修　川上デザインルーム
　　　担当／川上元美　割田淳一　山崎佳子

照明　LIGHTING PLANNERS ASSOCIATES
　　　担当／面出薫　窪田麻里　村岡桃子　木村光

サイン　廣村デザイン事務所
　　　担当／廣村正彰　中村一行　宇津木幸治

ランドスケープ　マインドスケープ
　　　担当／柳原博史　大西瞳　清水拓郎　三好あゆみ

展示基本設計・実施設計
　　　トータルメディア開発研究所・凸版印刷共同企業体
　　　担当／水間政典

設計協力
　　　山岸建築設計事務所
　　　担当／半本隼也　齋藤しのぶ

　　　atelier A5
　　　担当／清水貞博　松崎正寿　清水裕子

土木　日本海コンサルタント
　　　担当／中田匡

地質調査　エオネックス

積算　舘建築積算事務所
　　　担当／舘厚志　舘昌宏　舘拓希

防災　明野設備研究所
　　　担当／土屋伸一　北堀純

音環境計画協力　明治大学
　　　担当／上野佳奈子

サイン基本計画協力
　　　担当／岩松亮太

施工 ───────────────────

建築　清水・豊蔵・表・寺井・双建特定建設工事共同企業体他
　　　担当／亀井優　岡本正樹　紺谷治　林憲　上條浩一

　　　トーケン・ムラジ建設特定建設工事共同企業体
　　　担当／赤井雄伍　厚見吉亮

　　　岡・長坂特定建設工事共同企業体
　　　担当／元谷郷志　新裕司

　　　橘・兆建特定建設工事共同企業体
　　　担当／津田正之　田中勝

　　　和泉・大日土建 特定建設工事共同企業体
　　　担当／川元喜行　中島喜一郎

電気　第一電機・成瀬電気・ムラモト 特定建設工事共同企業体
　　　担当／新田誠実　金丸渉　寺本浩次

　　　柿本・ツボ・柴 特定建設工事共同企業体
　　　担当／廣瀬義隆　東谷卓史　坪田大輝　原佑輔

空調　菱機・三谷・松下 特定建設工事共同企業体
　　　担当／鈴木昭裕　野村尚広　寺西佑太

　　　柿本・第一電機・山森 特定建設工事共同企業体
　　　担当／小林壮大　田中暁大　林広樹

給排水衛生　鈴管・みなみ・ホクトー特定建設工事共同企業体
　　　担当／干場章司　小林寿　山本雅史

自家発電　米沢電気工事
　　　担当／中川雅賀　安達勝彦　宮崎護

融雪設備　テッククリエイト
　　　担当／澤田武一

展示　トータルメディア開発研究所
　　　担当／塩津淳司　青木優

サイン　ヨシダ宣伝

外構　北川建設　小山組　辰巳建設　邦和建設　毎田建設

　　　丸建道路　金沢舗道　辰村道路　吉田道路　加州建設
　　　三友工業　北川ヒューテック　沢田工業　島屋建設

　　　庭芸社　野々与造園　太陽緑化建設　中部緑地　兼六造園
　　　飛鳥緑地建設　昭美緑地　岸グリーンサービス　吉村植木園
　　　北川緑化工業　出島グリーン　駒谷造園

　　　ホクシン工業　日本海サービス

タイル　国代耐火工業所

屋根・板金　三晃金属工業

家具　アルフレックス ジャパン　イヨベ工芸社　内田洋行
　　　オカムラ　オリジン　カッシーナ・イクスシー　カンディハウス
　　　末永製作所　天童木工　日本ファイリング
　　　飛騨産業　山岸製作所　リアル・スタイル

ネットワーク工事　NTTデータ北陸

資料ICタグ　ソフエル

移転業務　図書館流通センター

規模

敷地面積　32,878.21㎡
建築面積　7,290.82㎡
延床面積　22,720.81㎡

本体建物
建築面積　5,950.66㎡
延床面積　22,272.78㎡

地下1階　6,311.62㎡
1階　5,356.12㎡
2階　4,629.60㎡
3階　4,907.46㎡
4階　1,060.36㎡
塔屋階　7.62㎡

建蔽率　22.18%　（許容：60%）
容積率　67.13%　（許容：200%）
階数　地下1階　地上4階　塔屋1階

寸法

最高高　18,532mm
軒高　14,182mm
階高　大閲覧空間（グレートホール）：18,500mm
天井高　大閲覧空間（グレートホール）：18,000mm

敷地条件

地域地区　都市計画区域内、市街化区域
　　　　　第二種中高層住居専用地域、高度地区、法22条区域
道路幅員　南17m
駐車台数　400台

構造

主体構造　S+SRC+RC　免震構造　一部CFT造
杭・基礎　直接基礎

設備

環境配慮技術
環境性能
BEI（省エネルギー性能指標）0.91
太陽光パネルの設置　10kW

空調設備
空調方式　中央熱源方式＋個別熱源方式
熱源　　　空冷モジュールチラー＋空冷ヒートポンプパッケージ

衛生設備
給水　受水槽＋加圧給水方式
給湯　局所式電気温水器
排水　自然重力方式、一部ポンプアップ方式

電気設備
受電方式　普通高圧6.6Kv　1回線受電方式
設備容量　3,000kVA
契約電力　1,000kW
予備電源　非常用発電機625kVA

防災設備
消火　スプリンクラー設備、屋内・屋外消火栓設備、ハロン消火設備
排煙　加圧式機械排煙（階段室のみ）、その他自然排煙
その他　非常照明設備、避難誘導灯、非常放送設備、自動火災報知設備
昇降機　乗用エレベータ（15人乗り）×4台、（20人乗り）×1台
　　　　小荷物昇降機×2台、エスカレータ×2台

工程

設計期間　2017年9月～2019年6月
施工期間　2019年10月～2022年6月

工事費

総工費　約1,5000,000千円

外部仕上げ

本体建築
屋窓屋根　ステンレス鋼板t=0.4mmフッ素樹脂塗装
　　　　　シーム溶接
屋階屋根　押さえコンクリート
外壁　　　せっ器質タイル（レール工法）、
　　　　　コンクリート化粧打ち放し＋カラークリア塗装、
　　　　　ECP＋カラークリア塗装
開口部　アルミ建具、スチール建具、ステンレス建具、木製建具
軒裏　　ケイ酸カルシウム版
　　　　合成樹脂エマルションペイント塗装
ポーチ・テラス
　　　　600角タイル張り、木材・プラスチック再生複合材
屋外広場　インターロッキング、自然石
歩道　　瓦コンクリート

外構建築
屋根　溶融亜鉛アルミ合金めっき鋼板折版葺き
天井　県産杉板ルーバー
床　　瓦コンクリート

内部仕上げ

グレートホール
床　　能登ヒバフローリング t=12mm
壁　　コンクリート打ち放し化粧仕上げ
　　　カラークリア仕上げ杉板張り t=15mm
天井　県産杉板ルーバー t=15mm

屋内広場
床　　600角タイル張り
壁　　プラスターボード t=9.5mmの上、珪藻土仕上げ塗料
天井　県産杉板ルーバー t=15mm

あとがき
Afterword

石川県立図書館は2022年7月16日にオープンした。私たちが設計プロポーザルで設計者として選定されたのは2017年8月である。そして9月に基本設計が始まり、実施設計が完了したのは2019年6月、工事が始まったのは2019年秋である。設計から竣工まで5年を要している。また、その前に県が本図書館の建設を構想したのは2016年のことであり、構想からオープンまで6年の歳月がかかっている。建設時期はちょうどコロナの流行もあり、大変難しい状況にあった。

そのように長い年月をかけ、様々な困難があったからこそ、どのようにこの建物ができたのかを伝えていきたいという思いから、この本を考えたのは2022年8月頃である。建築画報社にお願いし、できれば22年中につくろうと思ったのだが、デザイナーの川上元美氏やグラフィックデザイナーの廣村正彰氏と相談して、構成がまとまったのが22年11月頃である。その時の出版目標は23年5月頃だったが、次々に新しいアイデアが出て、結局11月まで延びてしまった。

本書はこの図書館建設に関わった設計、デザイン、建設関係者の協力によって出版したいと考え、多くの方々に呼びかけてつくられた。このようなかたちで建設の記録がつくられる例はそう多くないと思われるが、ご協賛いただいた方々には深く感謝したい。

また、この本に登場しなかった本当に多くの方々の力で、本図書館はつくられた。特にお名前を挙げると、前石川県知事・谷本正憲氏、担当部局の水野裕志参与、畝本秀一参与にはクライアントとして適切なご指示をいただいた。また、設計段階では香山壽夫教授、故・竺覚暁教授、折戸晶子氏には丁寧なるご助言をいただいた。深謝したい。

設備設計では建築設備設計研究所、行政協議等に地元の山岸建築設計事務所、日本海コンサルタント、監理ではインテグラの村井祐二氏に大変お世話になった。ここに感謝を申し上げたい。その他、お一人お一人の名前を挙げることが難しいが、本当に多くの皆様のご協力のおかげで、この図書館はできた。私の師である金沢が生んだ偉大な建築家、谷口吉郎先生の言葉を借りれば世阿弥の「一座建立」である。

本書の制作は建築画報社の櫻井ちるど社長、編集部の宮崎励さん、そして環境デザイン研究所の仙田順子社長の支援のおかげである。また、長年の友人である川上元美氏と一緒に仕事ができ、藤塚光政氏に迫力のある写真を撮っていただき、美しいブックデザインに廣村正彰氏がまとめてくださったことは大きな喜びである。本書が今後の地域図書館づくりに貢献することを祈りたい。

環境デザイン研究所会長　仙田 満

The Ishikawa Prefectural Library opened on July 16, 2022. Its design proposal, in which we were selected as the designers for the project, took place in August 2017. The schematic design began in September, the detailed design was completed in June 2019, and construction began in the fall of 2019, taking five years from design to completion. The prefecture's plan to build a library was made even earlier, in 2016, and therefore it took a total of six years from its conception to opening. The COVID-19 pandemic hit during the construction, making things very difficult.

Precisely because of the long time we spent and the many difficulties we overcame, the idea of this book arose around August 2022, with the hope of conveying how this library was created. My original plan was to publish the book from Kenchiku Gahou Inc. by the end of 2022, but after consulting with designer Motomi Kawakami and graphic designer Masaaki Hiromura, the composition of the book was finally determined in November 2022. At that time, we aimed to publish the book in May 2023, but new ideas kept coming up one after another, and the publication was pushed back to November.

We sought the cooperation of many people, in order to produce this book with those involved in the design and construction of the library. This is not a common way of documenting the creation of an architectural work, and we are deeply grateful to all who have supported the publication.

In addition, many people who are not mentioned in this book contributed to the creation of the library. To name a few, the former Governor Masanori Tanimoto, and advisors Hiroshi Mizuno and Shuichi Unemoto of the Ishikawa Prefectural Government gave us appropriate instructions as our clients. Professor Hisao Kohyama, the late Professor Kakugyo Chiku, and Ms. Akiko Orito provided careful advice in the design stage. I would like to express my deepest gratitude to them.

Other major contributors include Kenchiku Setsubi Sekkei Kenkyusho, which participated in the facility design, Yamagishi Architects + Engineers and Nihonkai Consultant Co., Ltd., both local architectural firms that joined mostly in the administrative meetings, and Mr. Yuji Murai of INTEGRA, who was involved in supervision. I would like to express my gratitude for their great help and support. I cannot name each and every one of the contributors here, but this library was made possible thanks to the cooperation of so many people. Using a phrase from my mentor Yoshiro Taniguchi, a great architect of Kanazawa, this library was Zeami's *ichiza-konryu* (building a sense of unity between the host and the guest).

President Chirudo Sakurai and Rei Miyazaki of the editorial department of Kenchiku Gahou Inc., and President Junko Senda of the Environment Design Institute provided support for production of this book. It was also a great pleasure to work with my longtime friend Mr. Motomi Kawakami, and to use spectacular photos by Mr. Mitsumasa Fujitsuka with a beautiful book design by Mr. Masaaki Hiromura. I hope this book will contribute to the future development of local libraries.

Mitsuru Senda, Chairman, Environment Design Institute

協賛（50音順）
Sponsors

特別協賛

清水建設 株式会社

協賛

株式会社 オカムラ

有限会社 川上デザインルーム

株式会社 トータルメディア開発研究所

株式会社 図書館流通センター

日本ファイリング 株式会社

協賛

株式会社 イヨベ工芸社	株式会社 エオネックス
株式会社 柿本商会	有限会社 金箱構造設計事務所
株式会社 国代耐火工業所	三晃金属工業 株式会社
株式会社 末永製作所	株式会社 豊蔵組
飛驒産業 株式会社	株式会社 山岸製作所
リアル・スタイル 株式会社	

協賛

株式会社 アイテックムラモト	飛鳥緑地建設 株式会社
株式会社 アルフレックス ジャパン	株式会社 内田洋行
株式会社 NTTデータ北陸	オリジン 株式会社
株式会社 カッシーナ・イクスシー	株式会社 金沢舗道
株式会社 カンディハウス	株式会社 岸グリーンサービス
柴電気工事 株式会社	有限会社 昭美緑地
株式会社 ソフエル	第一電機工業 株式会社
中部緑地 株式会社	株式会社 出島グリーン
株式会社 天童木工	株式会社 野々与造園
ホクトー 株式会社	三谷産業 株式会社
ヨシダ宣伝 株式会社	米沢電気工事 株式会社
菱機工業 株式会社	

写真クレジット	藤塚光政	表紙, 2-3, 6, 7, 30-35, 48-51, 55-57, 72-75, 77, 90-94, 96-98, 99(下), 116(上), 117-119, 136-137, 141
	エスエス北陸支店	8-9, 60, 62, 65, 66, 69, 102, 104, 107-109, 111, 113
	大倉英揮（黒目写真館）	95, 99(上)
	ナカサアンドパートナーズ	4-5, 52-54
	小寺 恵	16, 18, 21, 25, 27-29, 38, 42, 44, 46, 70-71, 76, 80, 83, 84, 89, 114-115, 116(下), 122, 125, 126, 131, 133
	清水貞博	134-135
	柳原博史	138-140

編集協力・資料提供　　金箱構造設計事務所、清水建設、ライティングプランナーズ アソシエーツ、廣村デザイン事務所、川上デザインルーム、
　　　　　　　　　　　マインドスケープ、atelierA5建築設計事務所、環境デザイン研究所

取材・撮影協力　　　　石川県立図書館

めぐる、めくる、めくるめく
石川県立図書館の新世界

Explore, Encounter, Experience
Discovering the World of Ishikawa Prefectural Library

2023年11月16日　初版第一刷発行

編著　仙田 満＋環境デザイン研究所

発行　建築画報社
　　　東京都新宿区新宿2-14-6
　　　TEL 03-3356-2568
　　　www.kenchiku-gahou.com

装丁・デザイン　廣村デザイン事務所

翻訳　フレーズクレーズ

印刷・製本　山田写真製版所

ISBN978-4-909154-72-9　C3052